Springboards For Teaching

IMAGINEERING

A "Yes, We Can!" Sourcebook for Early Technology Experiences

BILL REYNOLDS
BOB CORNEY
NORM DALE

Trifolium Books Inc.
TORONTO, CANADA

Trifolium Books Inc.
250 Merton Street, Suite 203
Toronto, Ontario, Canada, M4S 1B1
Tel: 416-483-7211 Fax: 416-483-3533
E-mail: trifoliu@ican.net

Special Note: This resource has been reviewed for bias and stereotyping.

Canadian Cataloguing in Publication Data

Reynolds, Bill 1948–
Imagineering: a "yes, we can!" sourcebook for early technology experiences

(Springboards for teaching)
ISBN 1-895579-19-8

1. Technology—Study and teaching (Primary). 2. Design, Industrial—Study and teaching (Primary). 3. Technology—Study and teaching—Activity programs. 4. Design, Industrial—Study and teaching—Activity programs. I. Corney, Bob, 1934– . II. Dale, Norm. III. Title. IV. Series.

LB1594.R48 1998 372.3'58044 C98-932137-1

Project Editor: Jon Bocknek/James A.W. Rogerson
Design, layout, graphics: Heidy Lawrance Associates
Project coordinator: Rodney Burke
Production coordinator: Heidy Lawrance Associates
Cover design: F1333 Design Inc.

Trifolium Books Inc. acknowledges with gratitude the generous support of the Government of Canada's Book Publishing Industry Development Program (BPIDP).

Printed and bound in Canada
10 9 8 7 6 5 4 3 2 1

Trifolium's books may be purchased in bulk for educational, business, or promotional use. For information, please write: Special Sales, Trifolium Books Inc., 250 Merton Street, Suite 203, Toronto, Ontario, M4S 1B1

Safety: The activities in this book are safe when carried out in an organized, structured setting. Please ensure you provide your students with specific information about the safety routines used in your school. It is, of course, critical to assess your students' level of responsibility in determining which materials and tools to allow them to use.

Note: If you are not completely familiar with the safety requirements for the use of specialized equipment, please consult with the appropriate specialty teacher(s) before allowing use by students. As well, please make sure that your students know where all the safety equipment is, and how to use it. The publisher and authors can accept no responsibility for any damage caused or sustained by use or misuse of ideas or materials mentioned in this book.

TABLE OF CONTENTS

Meet the Authors vi

Preface: How Does Technology Fit In? viii

Getting Ready 1

What's the Value of Technology Education for Young Children? 1

N.I.C.E.: A Simple Model for Problem-Solving 3

Materials and Tools You'll Need 8

How to Make Simple Structures and Mechanisms 13

How to Make...

Joinings 13

Hinges 14

Wheels 15

Cranks and Cams 17

Levers and Pulleys 17

Gears 18

Power Using Elastic Bands 19

Power Using Pneumatic and Hydraulic Systems 19

Introducing ***Imagineering*** Activities 20

Unit 1: Communities 23
Activity 1A: Our Town 24
Activity 1B: Crossing Guard 26
Activity 1C: Huffin' and Puffin' 28
Activity 1D: Communicator 30
Activity 1E: Second Time Around 32
Activity 1F: Puddle Play 34
Activity 1G: Fair Play 36

Unit 2: Story Time 39
Activity 2A: Pied Piper 40
Activity 2B: King Arthur's Court 42
Activity 2C: Storyland Pageant 44
Activity 2D: Jack & the Giant 46
Activity 2E: A Towering Challenge 48
Activity 2F: Bear With Me 50
Activity 2G: Collectibles 52

Unit 3: Space 55
Activity 3A: Space Base 56
Activity 3B: Pick a Planner 58
Activity 3C: Blast Off! 60
Activity 3D: Moon Rider 62
Activity 3E: Shuttle Cockpit 64
Activity 3F: Star Games 66

Unit 4: Pioneering 69
Activity 4A: Toys Were Us 70
Activity 4B: Food For Thought 72
Activity 4C: Tool Time 74
Activity 4D: Weave Your Own Placemat 76
Activity 4E: Swap Shop 78
Activity 4F: Bank on It 80
Activity 4G: Cropping Up 82

Unit 5: Time 85
Activity 5A: Hickory Dickory Clock 86
Activity 5B: The Beat Goes On 88
Activity 5C: Backtracking 90
Activity 5D: Race Against Time 92
Activity 5E: Get There on Time 94
Activity 5F: Slower Than Molasses 96
Activity 5G: A Memory-Treasure Timeline 98

Unit 6: Family and Friends 101
Activity 6A: Sun Hat 102
Activity 6B: Goodies for Grandma 104
Activity 6C: Friendship Soup 106
Activity 6D: Greetings from the Heart 108
Activity 6E: Nothing To Do? 110
Activity 6F: Try Puppetry 112

Appendices 114
(1) Note to parents 114
(2) Additional Equipment You Can Make 115
(3) Recipes for Pioneer Cooking 116
(4) Approaches to Assessment 119

Great Resources 127
Ideas & Techniques 127
Communities 130
Family & Friends 131
Pioneering 132
Space 134
Time 135

Meet the Authors

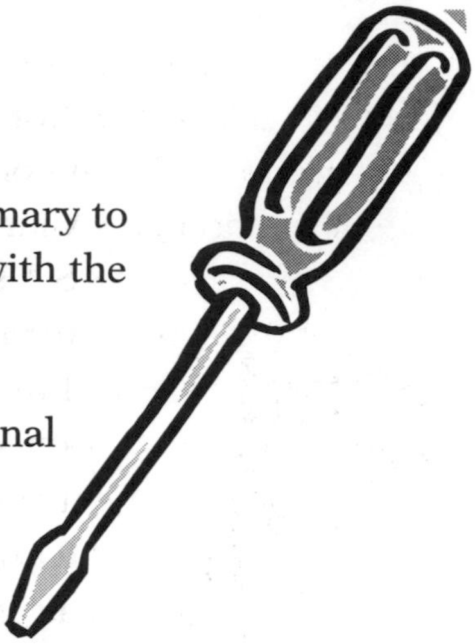

Bill Reynolds

In twenty years of teaching, Bill has taught classes from primary to senior divisions. As consultant for technological education with the York Region Board of Education, he began to promote technology activities in primary and junior classes. Since then, Bill has provided training and professional development for teachers and administrators across Ontario through faculties of education, conferences and PD workshops. As lead teacher for technology at Bogart Public School, a K–8 school with a technology focus, he provided leadership and technical training to help all teachers integrate design activities in their programs. Currently, Bill is Vice-Principal at Morning Glory Public School in Pefferlaw, Ontario.

Bob Corney

After 17 years in Wood-Patternmaking with The Steel Company of Canada in Hamilton, Bob obtained his teaching certificate from the University of Toronto and began teaching Cabinetmaking/Building Construction with the Wellington Board of Education. During this time, he obtained his Specialist Certification from the faculty at Queens University. The following and remaining years until retirement, Bob continued in Technological Education as a teacher, Technical Director, Consultant, and Coordinator for the Peel Board of Education.

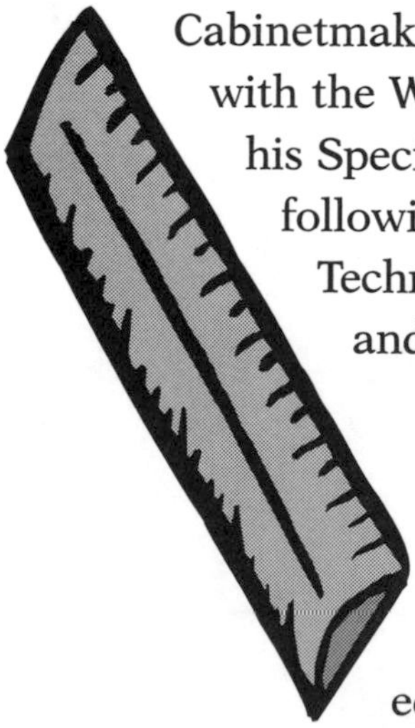

Currently Bob is a part-time instructor for OISE/UT, teaching in the Initial Certification Program for Technological Studies candidates, as well as a component of the Honours Technological Studies Specialist Qualification. He is also a partner with co-author Norm Dale in CorDale Enterprises, an educational consultancy with a focus on assisting elementary school teachers with the implementation of technology applications.

Norm Dale

Norm was born and raised in West-end Toronto, where he began his apprenticeship as a Construction Electrician and remained in the trade for ten years before entering the Faculty of Education at the University of Toronto. He taught Electrical Construction and Maintenance for 14 years. A one-year stint as President of District 14 O.S.S.T.F. was followed by 5 years at Frank Oke Vocational School as Chairman of Technological Studies. He went on to become the Consultant for Technological Education for the York Board, a position he retained until his retirement. During this time, Norm was involved in the creation of the Ontario Technological Education Coordinators' Council and served a two-year term as President.

Norm maintains his involvement with the application of technology in elementary schools, as directed by the Science and Technology Grades 1 to 8 curriculum guidelines, through his partnership with co-author Bob Corney in CorDale Enterprises.

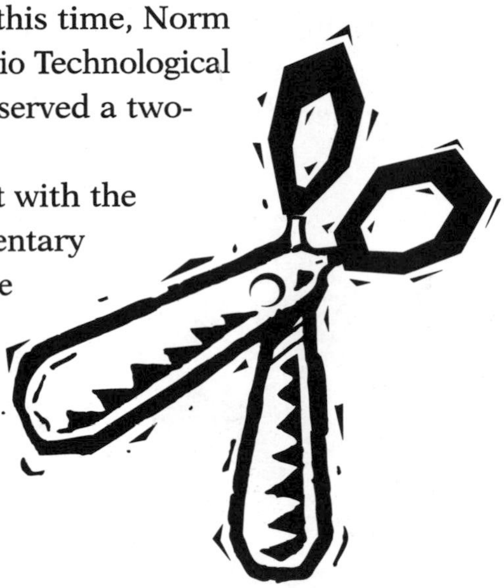

How Does Technology Fit In?

A question often asked by teachers of elementary programs is "how am I going to introduce my kids to technological problem-solving in an already jam-packed curriculum?" This is a valid concern and will only add to the anxiety unless the message is given that the technology component is not "as well as;" rather, it is "along with" and should be considered as integral—as enhancement and support rather than as a replacement of current curriculum directions.

Within existing curriculum, there are innumerable opportunities for students to acquire and practise technological problem-solving skills. These opportunities easily stem from

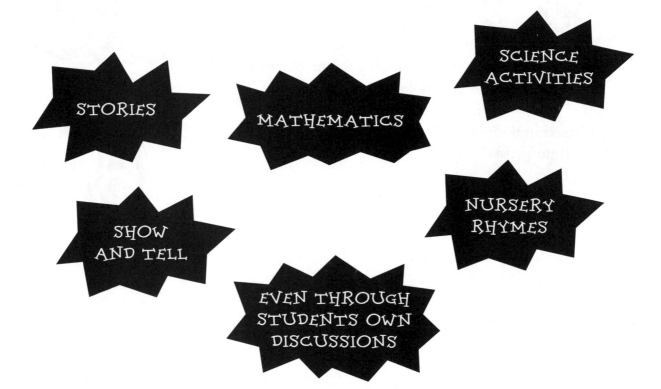

- STORIES
- MATHEMATICS
- SCIENCE ACTIVITIES
- SHOW AND TELL
- NURSERY RHYMES
- EVEN THROUGH STUDENTS OWN DISCUSSIONS

We urge you to incorporate the technological process into your day-to-day lessons at every opportunity. This book has been written to give you good ideas on how to do it successfully. We know that your students, their parents, and you, the teacher, will be pleased with the enhanced learning that results, as we have been over our years of teaching, using a technology integration approach.

Bill, Bob, and Norm
The Authors

Getting Ready

What's the Value of Technology for Young Children?

There are many definitions for technology. Traditional definitions deal with the use of tools and machinery connected with skilled trades or professional engineering. In educational circles, technology is often assumed to mean computers and their use. In a broader sense however, technology is more than tools. It is also a process which involves designing, creating, maintaining, and improving products that satisfy human needs.

Take the paper clip as an example. It is a device used to hold pages of paper together. It was designed to meet that need. It was a solution to the problem of loose paper—a precursor to the staple but with the environmentally friendly advantage of being reusable. Tools and machines were needed to produce it. Materials had to be refined to make the metal or plastic from which it was made. A long line of technological processes went into the creation of the paper clip.

And yet when need presents itself and imagination is given free reign the paper clip can also become another kind of tool. Have you ever unbent a paper clip and used it to reset a digital watch or clock? The straightened clip can act as a scraper for cleaning dirt caught in the frames of eye glasses or on window glass. When twisted it can be used to hang decorations. You have probably used paper clips for several other functions the authors have not considered. Human creativity used to modify our environment, including a paper clip, is technology.

So what's the value of engaging young children in technology education? Technology is all around us and it is changing the world in which we learn, work, and play at an ever increasing rate. Children need to recognize and use technology in creative and purposeful pursuits. More important, however, is the fact that technological activities help develop many transferable skills. These include problem solving, literacy, numeracy, teamwork, critical thinking, communicating, and positive attitudes such as persistence, adaptability, responsibility, initiative, self-esteem and self-confidence. Young children have a natural curiosity and inclination to experiment with materials and tools. Their naive and thus uncensored imagination combined with an inherent proclivity to do things with their hands makes them natural technologists or *imagineers*. By building on this innate disposition we take advantage of a natural motivation to learn. Technological problem-solving activities lead to enhanced learning and greater student success. What's more, students think it is great fun!

N.I.C.E.: A Simple Model for Problem Solving

What Is It?

In order to teach children *how* to solve problems we typically break the process involved in solving them down into a series of stages or steps. We do this for various problem solving activities including mathematical problem solving and social conflict resolution. The models provide a framework which can be applied to different problems and in different situations in order to find successful solutions. Models also provide a formal opportunity in which the solutions are reflected upon or analyzed to determine the extent of their success.

A variety of models for the technology process have been developed for use in schools. Each model establishes an arbitrary number of steps that is applied to the process of technological problem solving. In most the process starts with the recognition of a situation, need, or problem, and ends with an analysis of the solution by relating it back to the initial cause of the process. Some models are comprised of as many as 20 or more steps. Many have been based on industrial design concerns such as economics, ergonomics, marketing and manufacturing, or production processes. We wanted to give you an easy, yet effective model.

The "nice" thing about the model presented here is its simplicity. The *NICE* model of problem solving is comprised of just four stages. It shows children that the reason for making things is to satisfy needs. It can be applied easily to many classroom activities as well as 'real world' needs. It has been used successfully with children at both K–3 and grades 4–6 levels. It makes sense to them and the acronym stays with the students because it's easy to remember (and that's nice!)

The *NICE* process involves recognizing the **N**eed, developing **I**deas to satisfy the need, **C**reating the solution and **E**valuating the results, both of product and process.

N.I.C.E.: A Simple Model for Problem Solving

NEED

Students identify or recognize a need that has arisen, either from their own experience, as a result of a story read or listened to in class, or as a result of discussion around a topic.

IDEAS

Students talk about different ways that may be used to address or satisfy the need.

CREATE

The students design and/or create a solution to the need.

EVALUATE

The students will look critically at their solution and reflect on how it meets the need.

The following activity on pages 4 and 5 shows you the basic format we have used for the activities included under each theme throughout this resource.

N.I.C.E.: A Simple Model for Problem Solving

EXAMPLE ACTIVITY 1:

Kermit Kapers

For Your Interest

There are seven families of frogs represented by 56 species found in North America. They occupy a place in the class of vertebrate animals (with toads and salamanders) between fishes and reptiles called amphibians. They differ from these other classes because although they begin life in water and breath through gills, as they grow to adulthood, they develop lungs.

These creatures are natural predators to many of the bothersome insects that annoy humans yet, ironically, frogs and toads are declining because of humans—our pollution and urbanization of the planet.

Children often engage in studies of frogs by capturing the tadpoles from ponds and keeping them in jars to watch them develop over a short period of time.

NEED
(what are we being asked to do?)

We need to make a model of a frog so that:

- we can learn more about them
- we can play with it
- we don't have to hurt living animals

IDEAS
(what ideas do we have for doing it?)

- **What materials could we use?**
  - construction paper
  - cardboard
  - plasticene
  - clay
  - papier maché
- **Can we make it move?**
  - walk
  - jump
  - swim
- **How big should it be?**
  - life size?
  - scaled up or down?
- **What will it need to look like a frog?**
  - legs
  - eyes
  - mouth
  - tail
  - what colour?

Sparking Interest

- Visit a pond or nature area.
- Read or tell a story about frogs.
- Show a video or movie about frogs.
- Display pictures of frogs.

CREATE

(how can we make it?)

- **What materials will you need?**
- **What equipment will you need?**
  - scissors?
  - a ruler?
- **How can we make the body? Legs? etc.?**
  - cut and paste paper shapes together
  - paste frog pictures on a small box
  - mold clay or plasticene into a frog shape
- **How can we make it jump or move?**
  - make it into a string puppet
  - use oval wheels
  - use an elastic band as a spring
  - use a piece of plastic tubing to blow air under it

EVALUATE

(how well did we do what we needed to do?)

- **Does your frog look real?**
- **Does it move like a frog?**
- **Is your frog different from the other ones made by your class? How?**
- **Could you make your frog better? How?**

Nicer...

Invite the class to make a frog pond area in which their frogs can be displayed. They might make lily pads or bull rushes for the pond. They may even wish to add some other wildlife.

POSSIBLE SOLUTIONS TO THE FROG CHALLENGE:

This model, made of cardboard and paper, rolls on wheels. The rear wheels are oval so the frog seems to jump as it rolls.

This model, made of cardboard, uses an elastic band as a spring. The frog is opened on the ground and the spring makes it jump as the paper is pulled together.

This model is made of clay. It has a string attached to allow it to be operated like a puppet.

N.I.C.E.: A Simple Model for Problem Solving

EXAMPLE ACTIVITY 2:

Preparing for Technology Experiences

For Your Interest

The NICE model can be used to organize your teaching area for technology activities, be it a regular classroom, library-resource centre, or dedicated science/technology room.

OTHER "IDEAS" OR "QUESTIONS" WE COULD THINK ABOUT

- *What resources can you get from the community?*
  - found materials like plastic jars and bottles, lids, wood, etc.
  - tools
  - hardware such as nails or screws
- *How will you store the resources?*
  - boxes or bins
  - closets or cupboards
  - under tables
  - on shelves

NEED

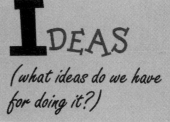

(what are we being asked to do?)

We need to organize the classroom resources and work areas to facilitate hands on technology activities so that:

- students can access a variety of materials and tools with which to build objects, artifacts, etc. to solve problems.
- students have room to manipulate the materials and tools safely.
- students can store away materials when not required.

IDEAS

(what ideas do we have for doing it?)

- **Which space can be utilized?**
  - A room (classroom, portable, art room, design & technology classroom, etc.) could be identified as a dedicated technology area for the division or school on an "as needed" basis.
  - An area within the classroom could be established as a technology centre.
  - A cart or kit boxes with materials and tools will be available for classes in the division or school to borrow on a needs basis.
- **What types of resources are available now?**
  - simple building materials like blocks
  - art supplies like scissors, glue, string, construction paper, clay, etc.
  - construction kits like Lasy, Lego, Construx, Meccano, etc.
  - simple tools such as hammers, screwdrivers, pliers, saws, etc.
  - work benches or sheet materials (masonite, plywood, etc.) to protect desks and tables

CREATE

(how can we make it?)

EVALUATE

(how well did we do what we needed to do?)

The answer here depends on the resources available to you and the grade(s) you teach.

Younger children, in kindergarten, are often involved in technology activities on their own. They mime or act out roles to model adult behaviours they have seen at home or in their neighbourhoods. When these children "play" in the classroom's activity centres whether it be with Duplo, clay, pots and pans, or hammers and nails they are solving problems by interacting creatively with technology. A teacher can build on these current activities to develop the children's awareness of technology.

- **Are the technology resources readily available to the students?**
  - Can they be put away quickly when not in use?
  - Is there enough room for the students to work safely with the tools and materials?
  - Could you improve the technology work area? How?

OTHER "CREATE" IDEAS

Although building toys are easy to integrate into a technology program, they are expensive. If the budget allows for the purchase of construction toys, Duplo, Lasy and Sono are excellent products to introduce technological concepts in junior and senior kindergarten and can be used throughout primary and junior division classes. Many students have had experience with Lego or Duplo at home or in daycare and are thus familiar with the basic components. Sets such as Teco, and Meccano are best suited to use in later primary division classes (Grades 2 and 3). Teco allows students to build large and functional models which develop the concepts of structures and machines. Meccano requires the use of tools (screwdrivers and wrenches) to join the component parts. Both of these kits have battery powered electric motors available to automate the models.

Most of the activities described in this resource can be done without expensive building kits. Ideas are presented in this chapter *(How to make simple structures and mechanisms)* which will empower students to develop workable technological solutions. They may be the basis for formal lessons or informal teacher interventions to help individuals or small groups through a design problem.

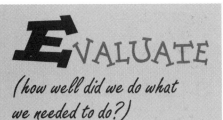

Materials and Tools You'll Need

Although it is possible to do all of the model making with paper, cardboard, scissors, and glue (or tape), the use of wood will add to flexibility in design and the stability of the structures. It encourages creativity while requiring the development of skills such as measuring and planning. Wood requires the use of different kinds of tools thereby broadening the students' skill development.

Teachers often acquire donations of scrap wood from the community. Usually the donations are in the form of off-cuts or leftovers from home renovation—bits of moldings, small pieces of lumber, etc. These donations are useful in many technology activities, but student solutions to problems are limited by the size and shapes of the pieces on hand. The number of cutting and shaping processes that primary children can do safely and effectively to this wood is limited.

Recently, however, some educational suppliers have introduced prepared wood products which are extremely useful in classroom design activities. The wood, 1 cm^2 (½" square) pine or basswood, is available in short lengths at a reasonable cost. Clear pine is a good wood for young students to use because it is soft. Basswood, if available, is better. Basswood is technically a hardwood but it is soft and stable to work with. Pine tends to warp and twist as it dries out. The wood can be cut and glued into square or rectangular frames. The frames can be assembled to make cubes or boxes. These three dimensional shapes can be used as basic building blocks to create just about anything the students can imagine.

Structures

Wood—1 cm^2 (½" square) is available from educational suppliers for classroom construction activities. It can be cut and glued to make frames which can be assembled into boxes.

Using frames and boxes, just about anything that you can think of can be built. Cover the frames with paper and paint to make houses, castles, toys, cars, trucks, and machinery.

Movement can be added to these models with wheels, hinges, levers, and pulleys. They can be powered *with elastics or controlled through air or water powered systems using syringes and plastic* tubing. (The fancy names for these systems are pneumatic and hydraulic systems. See page 19 for more information.)

Other materials that can be used in technology activities include: plasticine, stir sticks, bamboo barbecue skewers, paint, wood scraps, string, duct tape, bookbinding tape, masking tape, thumb tacks, binder clips, paper clips, play dough, etc.

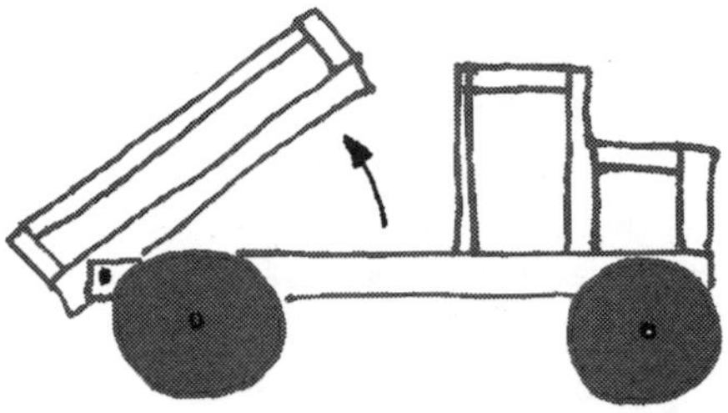

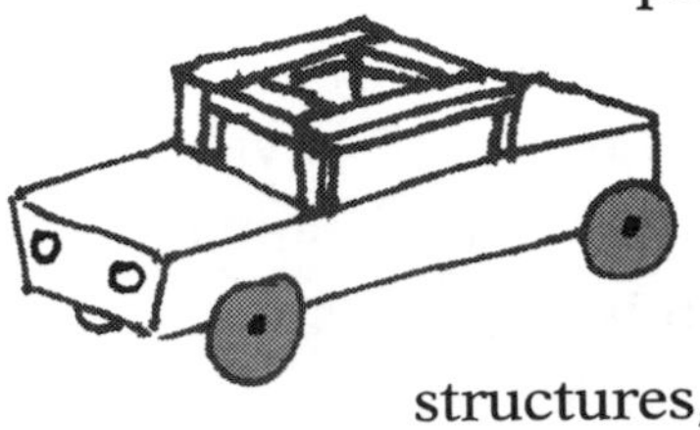

Regardless of the material used to make the basic framework of the structures, a wide variety of inexpensive, found material can be used to make the mechanisms. The form provided in the appendix identifies to parents many of the items needed by the class.

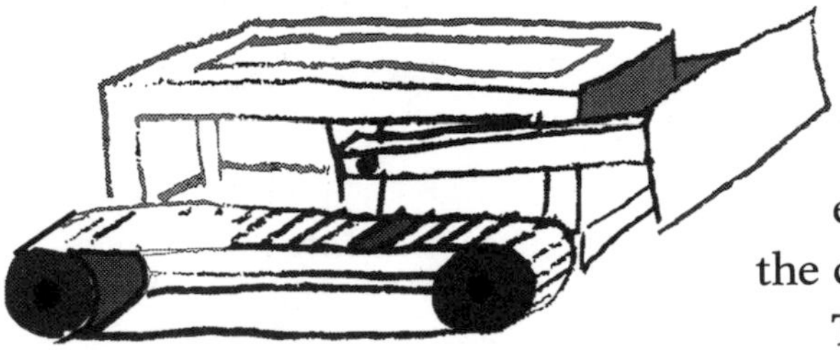

The tools required for the primary classroom are inexpensive and safe. When selecting tools for primary students, be sure to get tools with small handles. Small tools are easier for young children to hold and therefore safer for them to use. As well, these smaller tools are not as expensive as larger, professional grade tools.

Your basic tool kit will include saws, hammers, pliers, and a hand drill. There should be one saw for each construction centre or student group involved in a building activity. There should be one hammer for a centre or three to four shared in a whole class activity. Of all the tools the drill is the most difficult to supervise as it can make unwanted holes in desks in a matter of seconds. For this reason there should be only one drill in the construction centre and no more than two for a class.

There are three types of saws that could be used in a primary classroom: a **junior hacksaw**, a **dovetail saw**, and a **small back saw**. The junior hacksaw is the cheapest and easier to use of the three. These saws are available at any hardware store and through many educational suppliers.

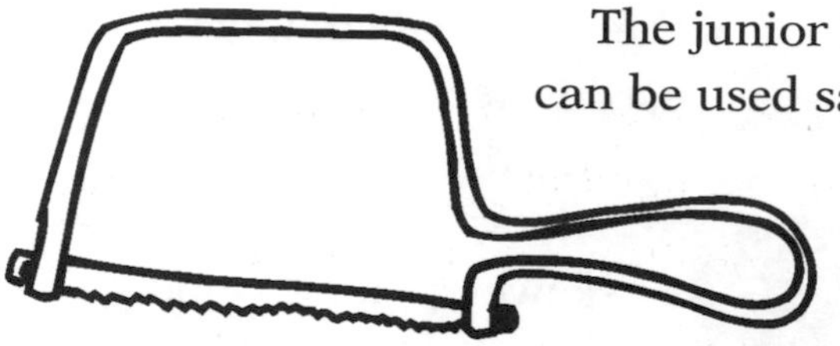

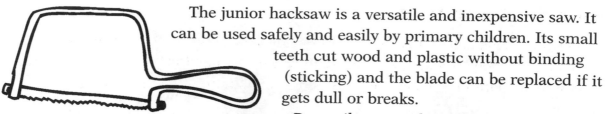

The junior hacksaw is a versatile and inexpensive saw. It can be used safely and easily by primary children. Its small teeth cut wood and plastic without binding (sticking) and the blade can be replaced if it gets dull or breaks.

Dovetail saws and small back saws are frequently available in schools. These saws can be used by primary children but are harder to manipulate due to their size and weight. They have larger teeth than the junior hacksaw making it harder to start a cut in wood and easier to cut a finger or hand. They should be used with a miter box and supervised carefully.

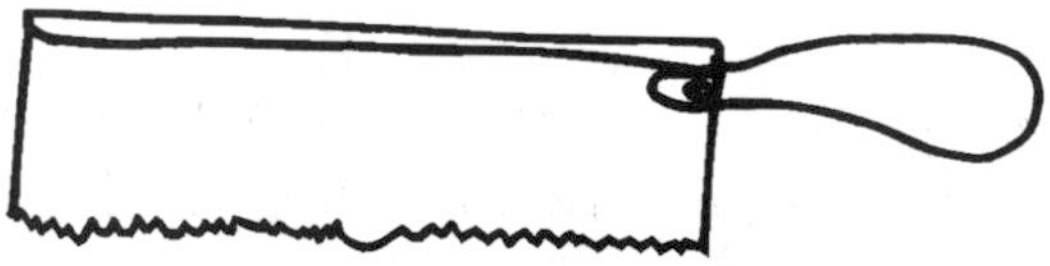

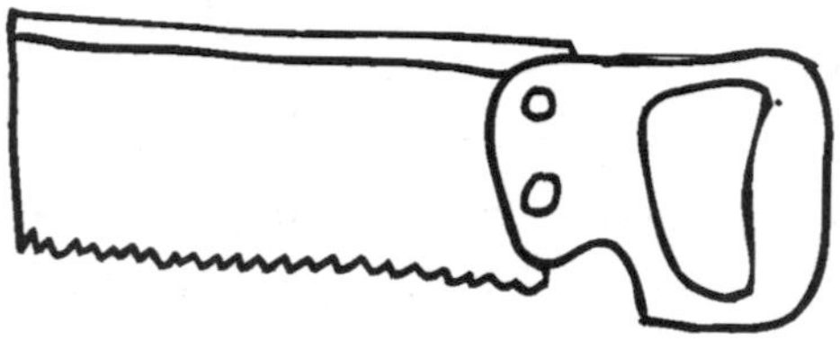

The saw should be used with a vise or a **bench hook**. Since vises are relatively expensive, the bench hook is an alternative used in many classrooms. Bench hooks can be purchased through some educational suppliers but are easy and cheap to make. Plans for a bench hook are included on page 115 in the appendix.

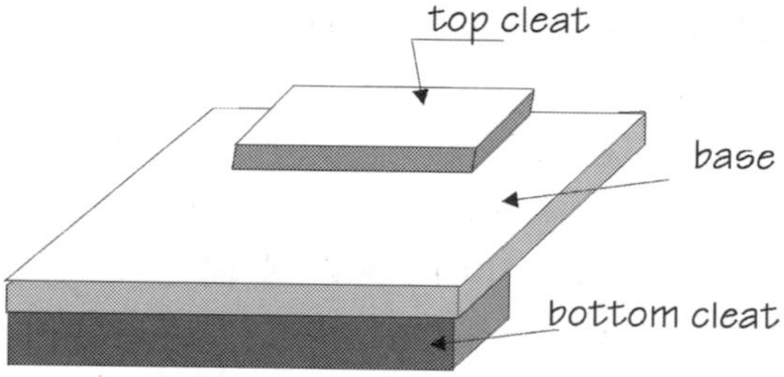

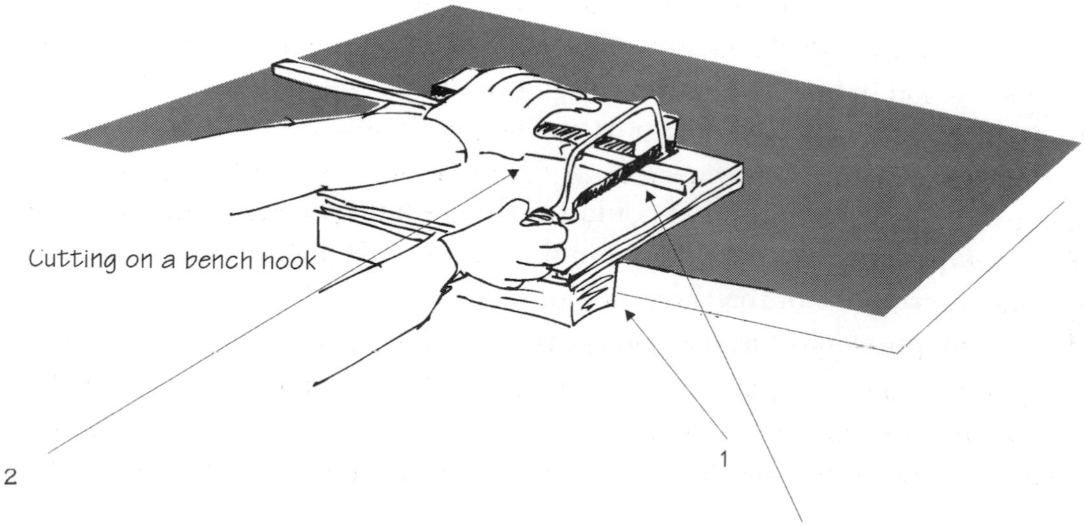

Using the Bench Hook

1. The bench hook is held tightly to the table or desktop with the bottom cleat touching the edge of the table or desk. It can be clamped in place with a spring clamp or C-clamp if the children have difficulty holding it while sawing.
2. The stock (material) which is to be cut is held against the top cleat with the thumb well back from the cutting end of the cleat.
3. The saw cut is made as close to the top cleat as possible so that when the blade passes through the stock it cuts into the base of the bench hook instead of the table top.
4. To cut—move the full length of the blade smoothly back and forth with light downward pressure. Too much force will cause the teeth to bind in the wood.

The hammer should be a light weight (7 oz.), steel shank, claw hammer. They are available through most hardware stores at very reasonable prices. Avoid the wooden handled hammer because the handle shrinks with changes in humidity and wear. This can cause the head of the hammer can come loose and possibly fly off the handle.

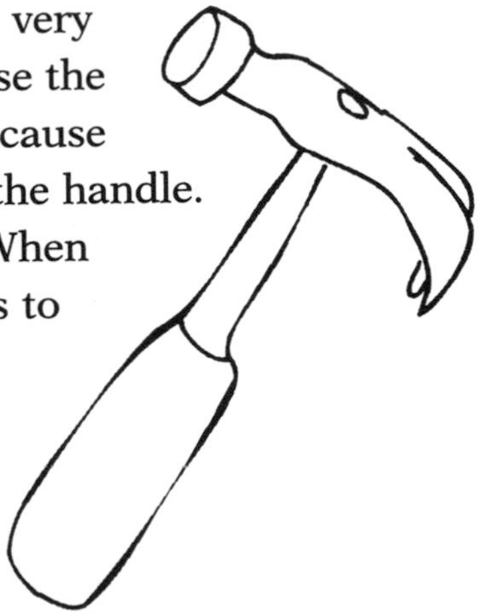

Small **claw hammers** are available at a reasonable cost. When children are hammering nails they should wear safety glasses to protect against chips of metal flying off the nails.

A **hand drill** is useful for making holes in wood, plastic and cardboard. The drill should be light enough for young children but sturdy enough to do the work. It should be able to hold a 6.5 mm (¼") drill bit. The drill requires drill bits. A set of small bits ranging from 3.18 mm to 6.5 mm (⅛"–¼") will provide the range of sizes necessary. Replacement bits will be required particularly for the smaller sizes. They break frequently as children learn to use the drill.

Although the hand drill is useful for making holes in plastic and wood, it can also make holes in desks and chairs unless its use is supervised carefully. Students should use a vise if possible to secure the material that they need to drill. Otherwise it should be held over the edge of the desk or table. Small bits of material are difficult to hold and drill. Whenever possible the hole should be drilled in a larger piece which can be cut to size afterwards.

Pliers are used to cut and bend wire. Inexpensive gripping/cutting pliers (called lineman's pliers) with 12 cm (5 inch) handles are available at any hardware store. Needle nose pliers are useful for reaching into tight spots and for making loops or eyes on the end or wire such as paper clips or coat hangers.

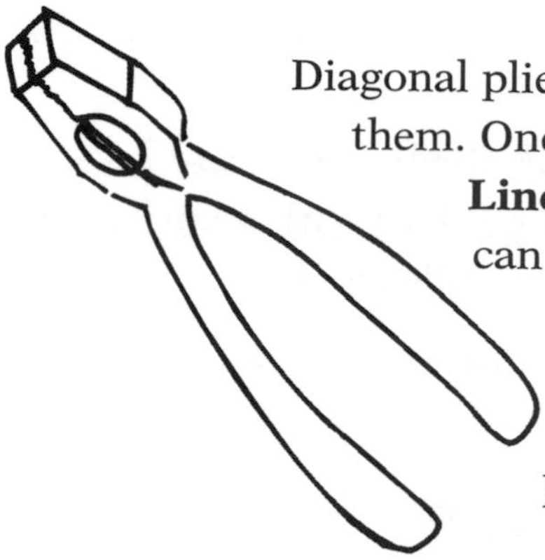

Diagonal pliers are strictly for cutting wire. There is no gripping part to them. One or two pair of each will serve the needs of the class.

Lineman's pliers are basic gripping and cutting pliers. They can be used for many operations including to hold small nails when hammering. They should not be used to cut nails. Their cutting edge is designed for softer wire. They can be used to cut coat hanger wire.

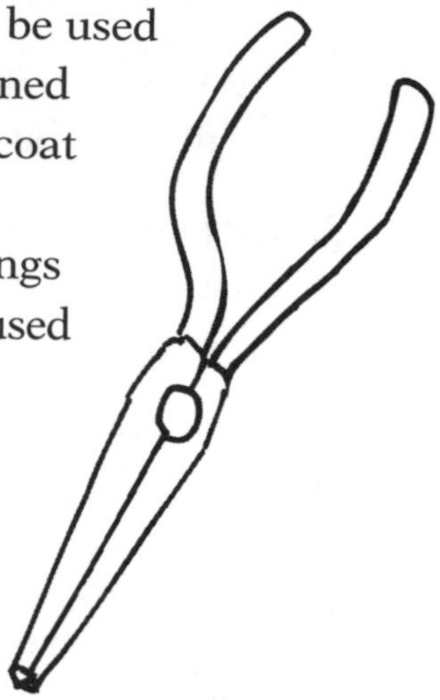

Needle nose pliers are used to grip things that are small or hard to get at. They should be used cautiously when twisting heavy wire, especially with inexpensive pliers, as the jaws can be bent out of alignment.

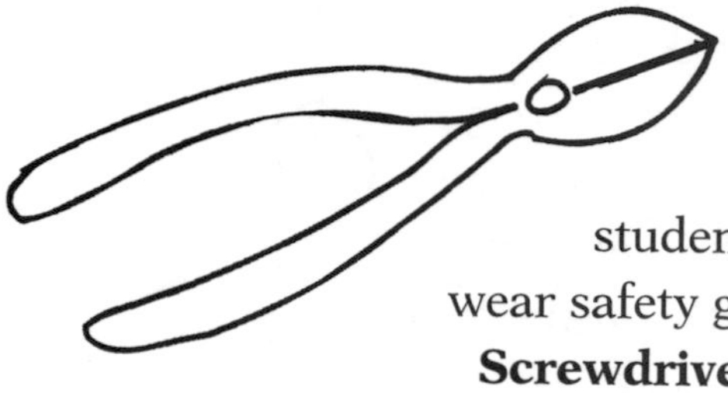

Diagonal pliers are designed to cut wire. They can be used when it is necessary to clip the wire close to a surface. Whenever students are cutting wire, they should wear safety glasses in case a small piece of wire flies off.

Screwdrivers come in a variety of sizes and types. Select drivers with small handles that the children can grasp easily. In most cases you will need **slot**, **Phillips** or star, and **Robertson** type drivers. For each type you will need a couple of sizes—1/8" and 1/2" for slot; #1 and #2 for Phillips; and green and red for Robertson. One set of screwdrivers should do for most activities.

There are many types of screwdrivers. Each type is used with a matching screw type. The most common is the slot type. The Phillips or star screwdriver is used in industry for everything from small appliances to automobiles. The Robertson driver is used extensively in building construction and is growing in popularity among woodworkers.

The size of the driver is determined by the size of the opening in the screw. It is important that the right size driver is used. Otherwise the screw head may be stripped or the driver damaged.

As your technology classroom develops, more tools may be added to extend the range of activities. Adjustable wrenches, nut drivers, jewelers screwdrivers, punches, etc., are just some of the tools you could add when needs arise and budgets allow.

How To Make Simple Structures and Mechanisms

A variety of solutions exist for every challenge in technology. Nobody knows all the answers, but through observation, experimentation and risk taking, good solutions can usually be found for most challenges. Diagrams in this chapter illustrate how to construct a variety of basic structures and mechanisms.

You may decide to teach some of the following ideas formally to the whole class. This would certainly be recommended for creating the basic joining method for simple structures. As children develop ideas for movement in their technological solutions, you may introduce the mechanics of hinges, axles, levers, etc., to small groups as their needs dictate. A background in mechanical engineering is certainly **not** a prerequisite to introducing technology. Proceed as you and your students' comfort level allows.

To use the following building technique, students should be able to measure accurately. Through trial and error students will learn the importance of accurate measurement. Structures depend on good joints for their strength and the strength of the joint depends upon how well the pieces fit together. This is especially critical when the solution the children develop is required to support some mass or withstand tension or compression from moving parts.

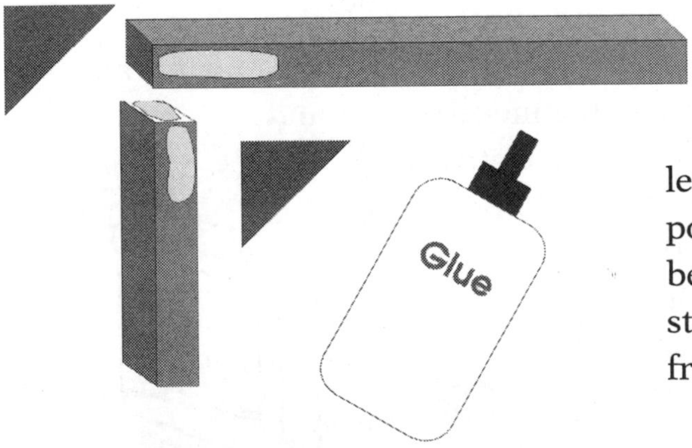

Joinings

Joints are glued with white glue or carpenter's glue, not nailed. This is less costly and easier for the students. If possible, a prototype of their model could be made from building kits like Lego. The students can then take measurements from the prototype.

Wood should be cut as square as possible. Triangles of Bristol board are attached to the joint to strengthen it. These are called gussets.

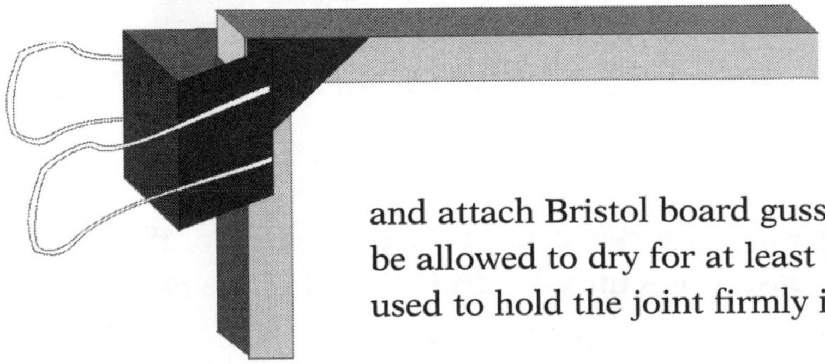

Apply white glue to wood and attach Bristol board gussets to each side. The joint should be allowed to dry for at least 20 minutes. Binder clips can be used to hold the joint firmly in place while glue dries.

Frames are created by making squares and rectangles. These can be assembled into three dimensional structures such as cubes or boxes.

Note: If possible, purchase carpenter's (yellow) glue. It forms more effective joints than white glue. It is stronger and sets faster.

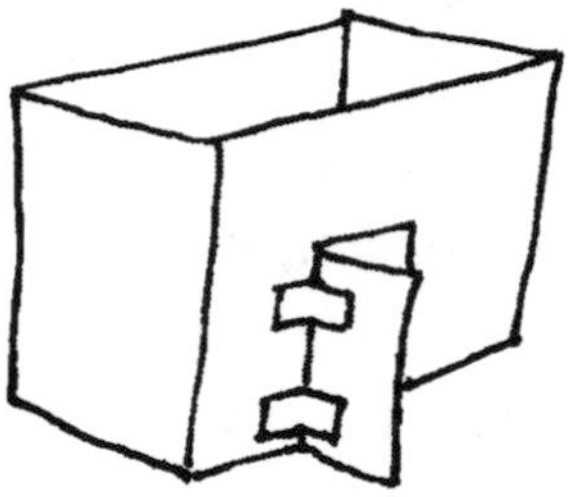

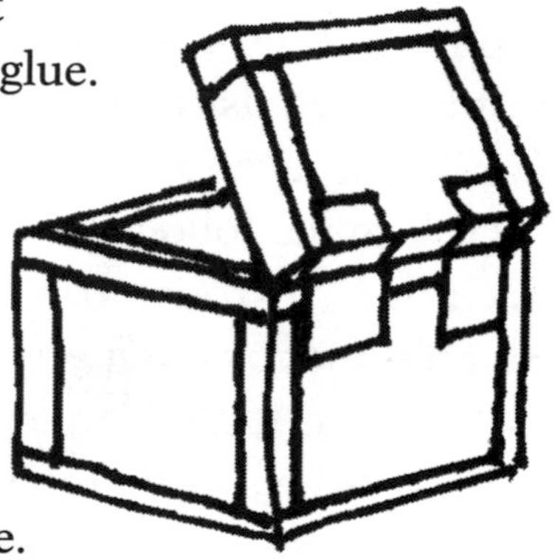

Hinges

Normally we think of hinges on doors. There are hinges on many objects besides doors. Hinges can be made simply by using tape. Fabric tape like bookbinding tape or duct tape works well to make a hinged joint.

Hinges can also be made using Bristol board tabs which are glued to the movable part and the stationary part of the structure. Bristol board will bend many times without tearing. Be careful not to put too much weight on the hinge though.

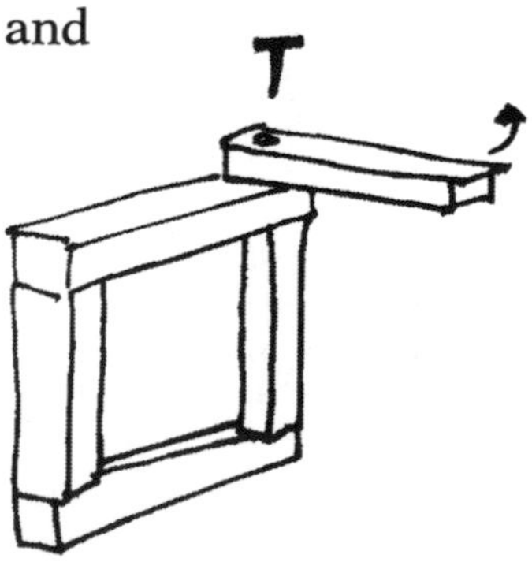

Hinges can be made using nails as a pin just like the hinges on doors. A hole, larger than the diameter of the nail, is drilled in the part that will move. The nail is then placed through the hole and hammered into the stationary part of the structure. As long as the nail is left slightly loose, movement will occur.

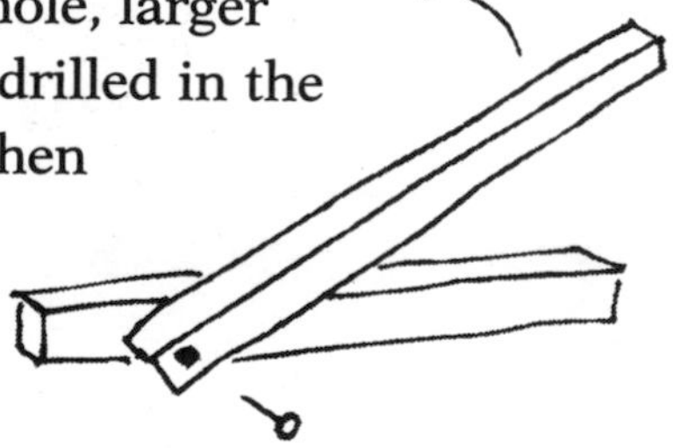

A barbecue skewer, coat hanger wire, or dowel could be used in place of the nail if a long pin is needed. In this case, holes must be drilled in all of the parts and the skewer, wire, or dowel is glued to either the movable part or the stationary part—BUT NOT BOTH!

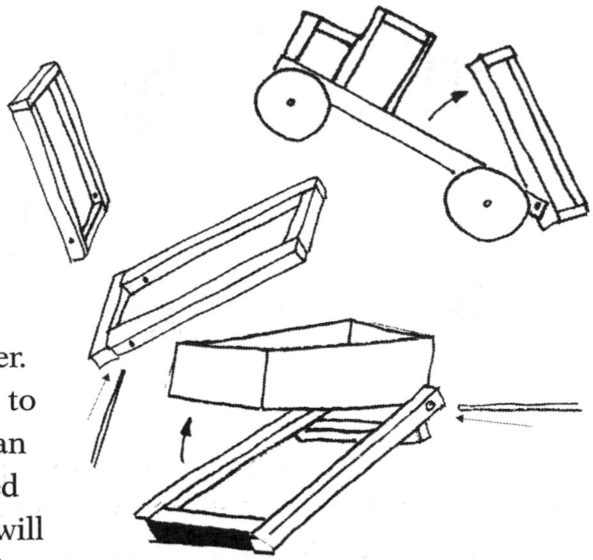

Wheels

Bottle and jar lids make excellent wheels. These should be collected and sorted to provide wheels of equal diameter. The centre of the wheel needs to be drilled or punched out for an axle. If the centre is not located accurately, the vehicle or toy will not roll smoothly. You can help students to locate the centre with the use a 45° set square and a right angle corner such as the inside corner of a drawer or the corner of a window frame.

Place the wheel tightly in the corner of the right angle. Place the set square in the corner as shown. Draw a line on the wheel along the 45° edge of the set square.

Rotate the wheel about 90° and draw a second line.

The intersection of the two lines is the centre of the wheel.

There are two ways to make wheels that turn. One way is to attach the wheel firmly to the axle and allow the axle to turn freely. The other method is to allow the wheel to spin on the axle. If both axle and wheel are fixed in place, neither will turn.

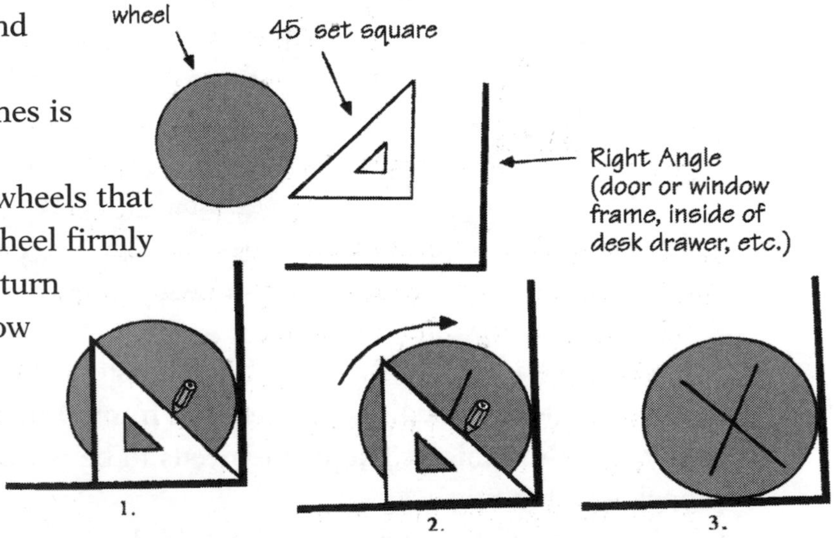

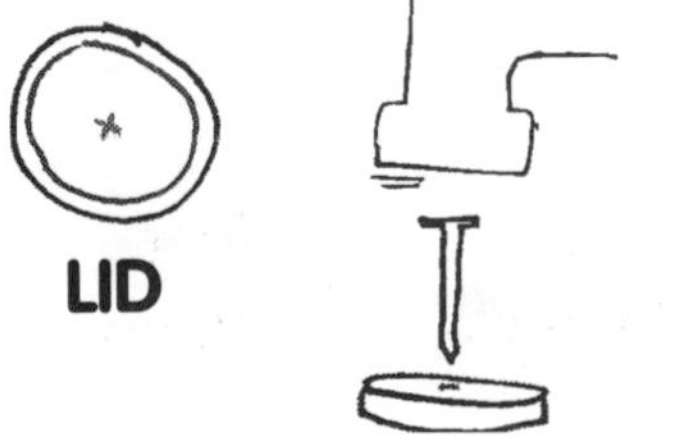

The size of the hole in the wheel will depend on how the wheel will be fastened to the axle. If the wheel and axle are both going to turn, the hole should be only as big as the axle. If the wheel is to spin on the axle, the hole must be larger than the axle.

Axles are the shafts that go through the middle of the wheels. Wheels turn on axles. Axles can be made with nails or tacks allowing each wheel to turn independently. They can also be made from dowels, barbecue skewers, or from coat hanger wire. The part of the wheel assembly that moves must overcome friction from the part that doesn't move. Where the friction occurs is called the bearing. Good bearings minimize friction.

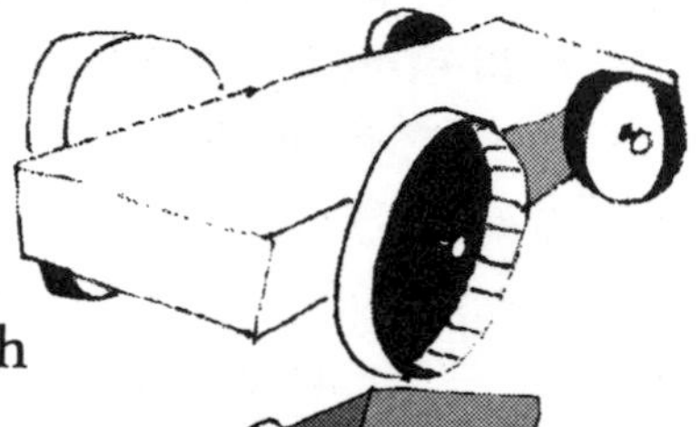

To make good bearings, the surfaces should be smooth and slippery.

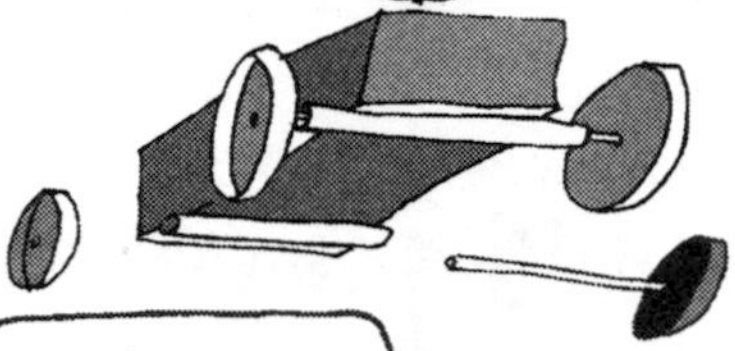

Fixed axles, the ones where only the wheels move, require the hole in the wheel to be smooth and round. These holes should be drilled.

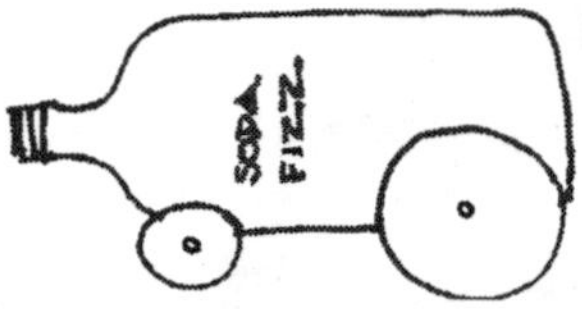

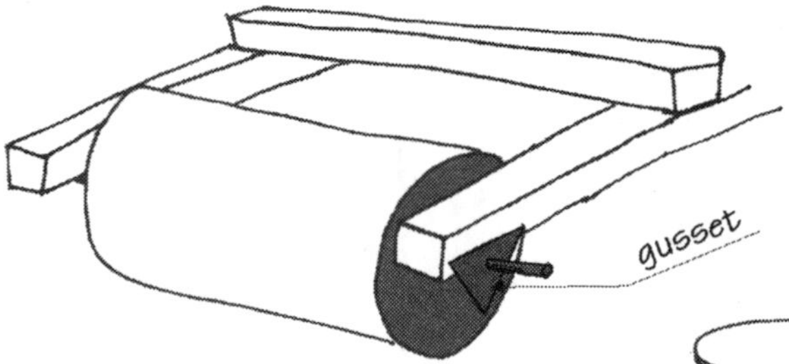

Rotating axles need to be free to turn easily. A large drinking straw, fixed to the vehicle provides a smooth bearing in which a dowel, skewer, or coat hanger axle can spin. Other ideas for bearings include large beads, clothes pegs, gussets with holes punched in them, or holes drilled through the vehicle's frame or body.

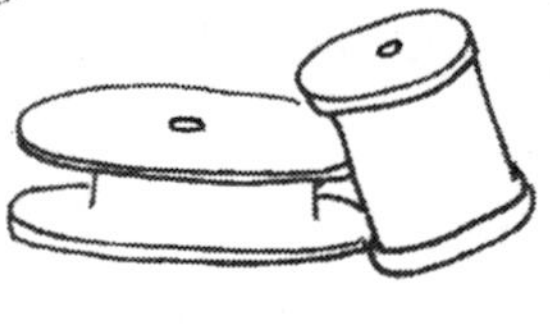

Anything that rolls can be made into a wheel. Tin cans, film canisters and spools make good roller wheels. These wheels are usually enclosed in a frame rather than being fastened on the outside of the vehicle. The frame needs to be constructed carefully to allow the wheels to fit inside.

If the top of the can or similar cylinder is missing or has a large hole in it, a disc of Bristol board can be fastened across it so that a centre hole can still be punched for the axle.

Notice the bearings in these diagrams. The tin can wheels use a gusset bearing and the spool wheels have clothes peg bearings.

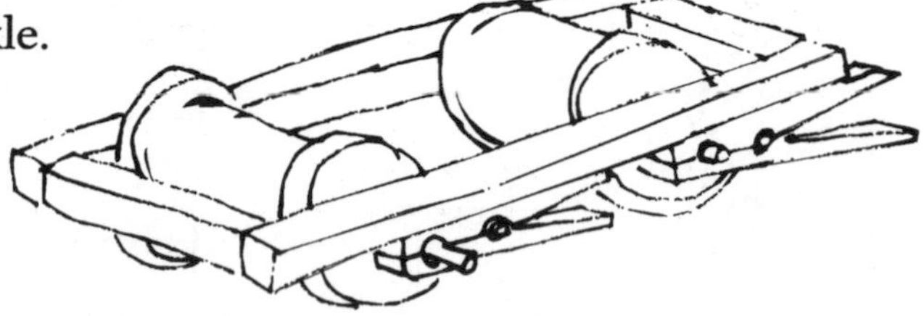

Cranks and Cams

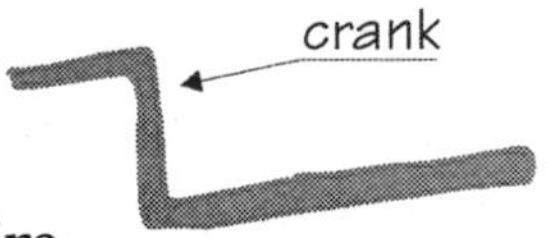

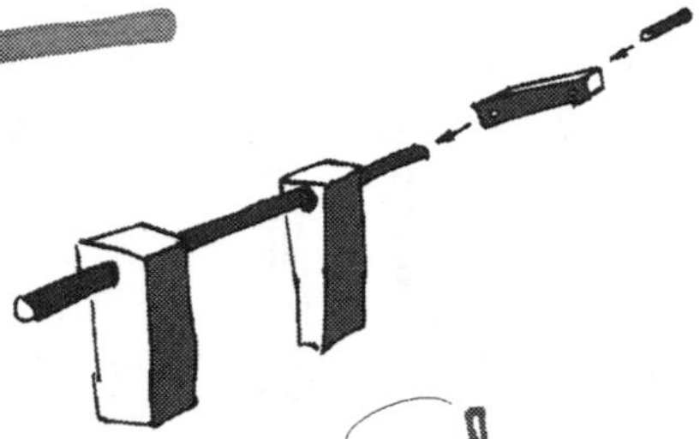

Cranks are mechanisms which make it easy to turn something. They can be made from wire or wood. The crank shaft must be supported in a bearing. The crank is a bent part at the end of a special axle called a crankshaft.

Cams are also bends in axles or shafts but this time the bend is in the middle of the axle. A cam moves up and down as the axle turns. This action can be used to make movement. If a cam is put in the axle of a wheel on a toy, the cam can cause some part of the toy to bob up and down as the toy rolls. In the picture below, the clown head starts in a low position. It moves up with the cam and wobbles back and forth as the wheels turn.

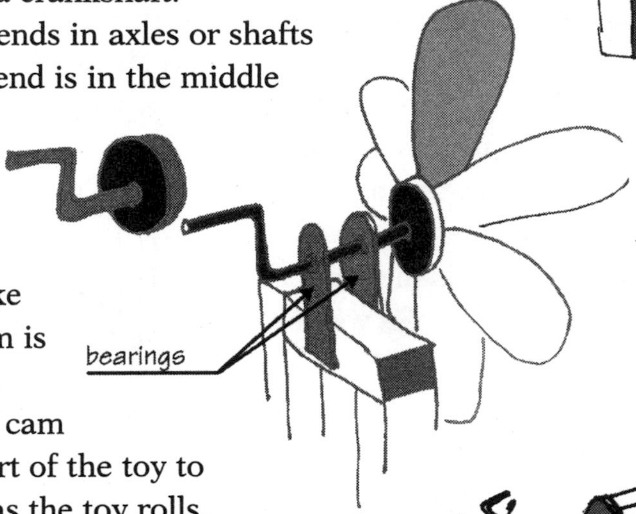

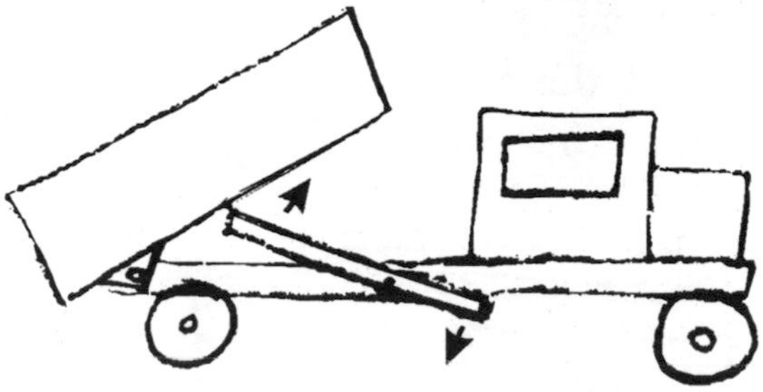

When the lever is pushed down, the box on the truck moves up.

Levers and Pulleys

Levers are relatively simple yet extremely important mechanisms. They are used to transfer an action from one point to another and to gain mechanical advantage (reduce the amount of force required to move an object). They often operate on an axle. Coat hanger wire or barbecue skewers

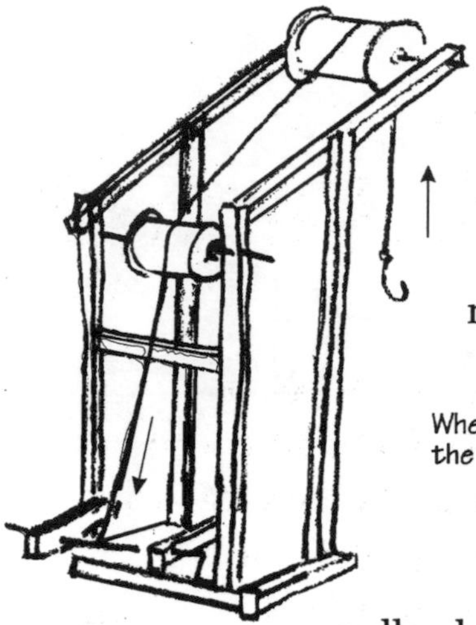
When the string is pulled down, the hook moves up.

work well. The lever must pivot on the axle so the hole through the lever must be larger than the axle.

Spools can be used for pulleys and winches.

A pulley is a simple machine that changes the direction of motion on a string, rope, cable or belt. Using multiple pulleys will reduce the amount of force required to lift a given mass. Pulleys can be used with elastic bands and battery powered motors to activate toys and models.

The winch is a special pulley because the string, rope or cable is attached to the spool and can be wound up or let down by a crank. This is the type of machine used to lift a bucket out of a well or to pull in a fish on a fishing rod.

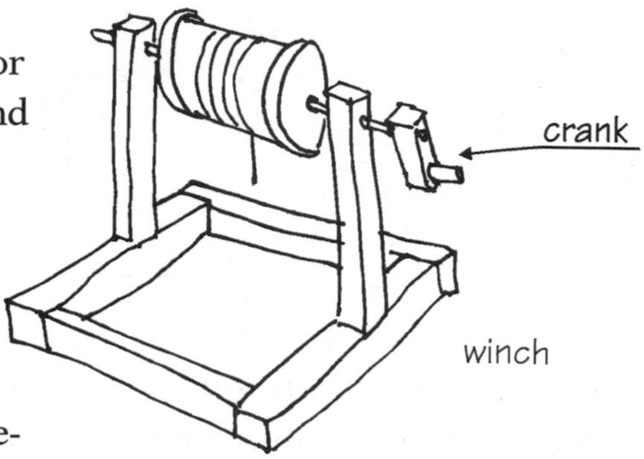
crank
winch

Gears

Gears are useful mechanisms for making movement. They can be made by gluing corrugated cardboard, like that used on bulletin boards, around spools or cylinders. The bumpy part of the cardboard should be facing out. If spools of different diameter are used, they will turn at different speeds.

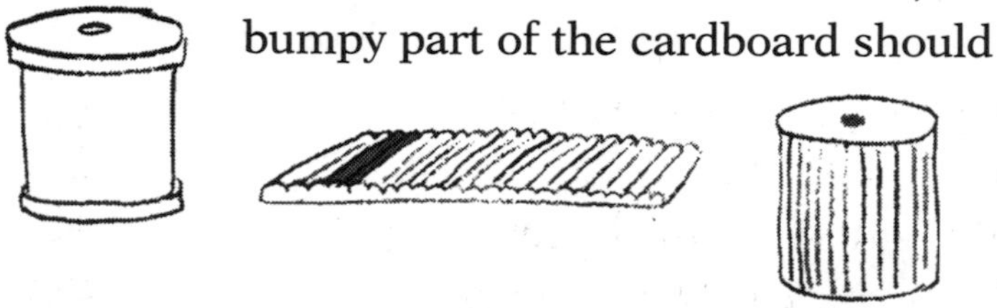

Gears turn in different directions when they mesh.

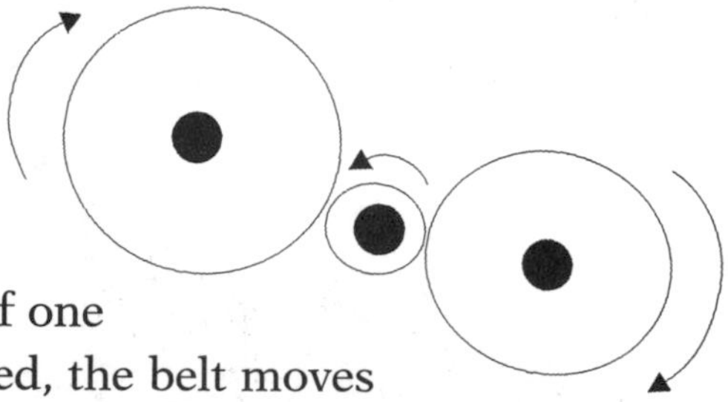

Gears can act like pulleys if they are connected by a belt. The belt needs to mesh with the teeth in the gears, so it is made from corrugated paper too. If one gear is turned, the belt moves and turns the other gears.

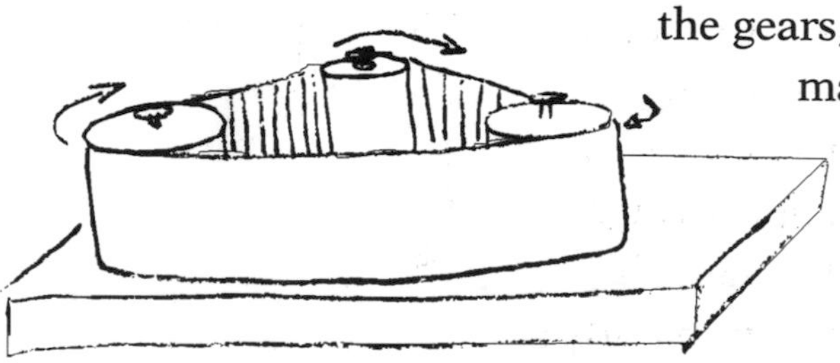

This time they all turn the same direction.

If the belt is turned with the teeth out it acts like the track on a caterpillar type vehicle.

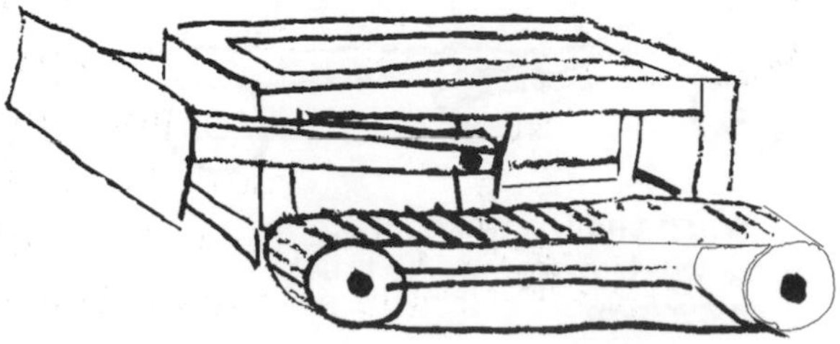

The belt can also be used as a conveyor belt if the gears are placed on their sides.

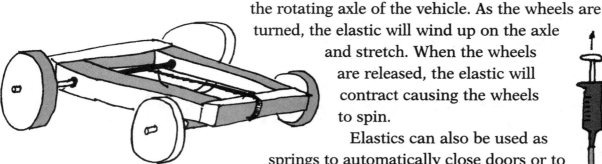

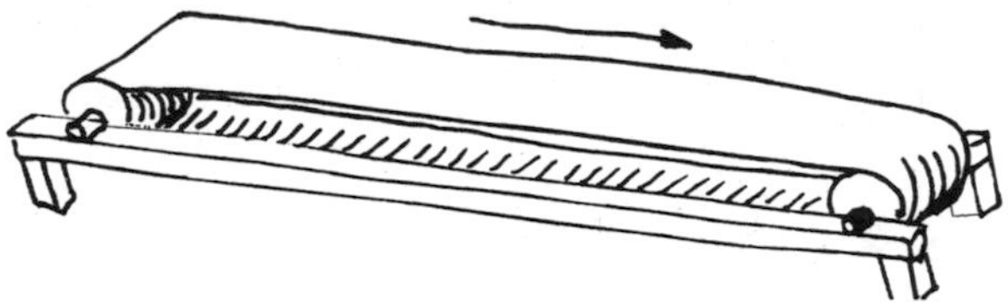

Power

• *Using Elastic Bands*

Elastic bands can be used to power vehicles. A long elastic band can be cut and one end tied to the body or frame of the vehicle. The other end is attached to the rotating axle of the vehicle. As the wheels are turned, the elastic will wind up on the axle and stretch. When the wheels are released, the elastic will contract causing the wheels to spin.

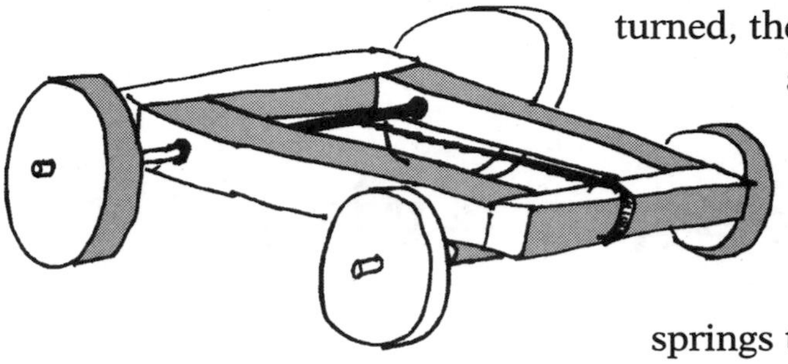

Elastics can also be used as springs to automatically close doors or to make levers spring up or down.

• *Using Pneumatic & Hydraulic Systems*

Pneumatic and hydraulic systems are used to power mechanisms from remote locations. Pneumatic systems use air as the driving force. Hydraulics use liquid (usually oil but in the classroom we'll use water). Two syringes connected with plastic tubing are used to make the system.

Before connecting the tubing, the plunger on one syringe must be pushed in all the way. The other must be out as far as it can go. If the syringes are different sizes, the larger syringe must have its plunger all the way in. The two syringes are then connected with the plastic tubing as shown.

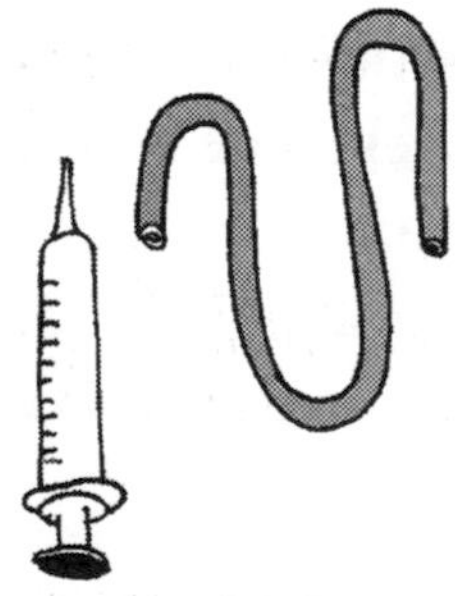

If a hydraulic system is to be used, assemble the complete system in a sink or bucket so that no air gets in the tube or syringes.

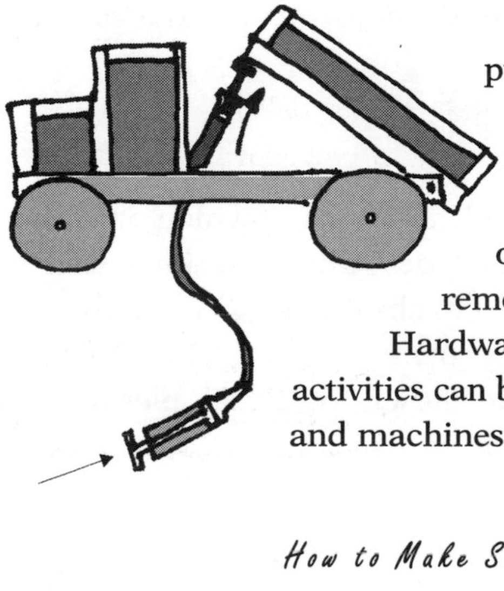

When the plunger is pushed on one syringe (the controller) the plunger on the other will extend. If the controller plunger is pulled out, the other plunger will move in. This is remote control.

Hardware and devices needed for the technology activities can be recovered by taking apart old toys, appliances and machines. The activity *Second Time Around* is designed to encourage children to take things apart so they can learn about mechanisms and also to increase the class supply of hardware.

Cautions & Safety

- ☑ Prior to their disassembly, cut the cord caps (plugs) off of any devices which could be plugged into electrical sockets.
- ☑ Students should not work on devices which contain picture tubes (TV's or computer monitors) or radioactive elements (smoke detectors). If in doubt as to the safety of an appliance in this centre, discard it.

Introducing Imagineering Activities

Communities

The communities theme enables primary students to relate to their neighbourhood. It should be adapted by each school to identify and highlight the important features of the students' own community. Many features will be common to all schools and some will be unique to the communities of a geographic area.

Regardless of the location of the community, there are many applications for technological problem solving. In the activities under this theme, students will think about some of the problems that can occur within a modern community and consider solutions to them. Traffic safety and waste reduction are technological issues that young people immediately understand. Structural technology can be investigated through science by comparing building materials and techniques. Mechanical technology is a major component of amusement park rides. Students will see through active exploration that design plays as significant a role in the functionality of our cities and towns as it does in the enjoyment of the games we play.

Story Time

Fairy tales and legends provide great settings and situations in which problems can be solved through technology. This theme includes some traditional tales and legends to provide examples that could be applied to almost any story. Even mother goose rhymes can lead to technological problem solving.

The tales that the activities are based on were chosen to be examples only. The need for a shield in the King Arthur activity could easily be applied to a story about dragons such as *The Paper Bag Princess*. Captain Hook's pirate ship could be the boat that takes Max to *Where The Wild Things Are*.

It is also possible to link themes through stories and show technology as both fanciful and practical. In other themes, activities have been based on incidents in *The Three Little Pigs* (Community) and *Goldilocks* (Family). The Pioneer theme can be linked to *Jack and the Bean Stalk* through planting and growing beans. With imaginations set free through fairy tale and legends students are able to generate ideas and solutions to needs in the most creative of ways.

Space

The Space theme includes flight, the solar system, and space travel. All of these topics can be explored through technological problem solving. This theme is a natural arena for developing technological projects.

Humans have always had a fascination with flight. The stories span from Icarus to Luke Skywalker. The reality of flight has developed from kites through balloons to powered flight. We have seen Earth from space and experienced seeing people walk on the moon and although there was no green cheese, our curiosity has not diminished.

Curiosity with flight and space is especially apparent in the primary classrooms. The investigation of these topics provide young students with a wealth of opportunities to explore and learn through technology. The activities within this theme include building space structures and machines, developing an awareness of space exploration dangers by designing a board game, etc. The activities draw on students vast knowledge of space (both fantasy and reality) and invite creativity in their solutions.

Pioneering

The pioneer theme is rich with opportunities for primary students to investigate technology. Activities in this unit can focus on making toys, building structures such as cabin or barns, designing wagons or other transportation related vehicles, mixing and cooking food such as quick breads, yeast breads or cookies, and designing and making simple musical instruments.

When possible, the class should visit a pioneer museum or display so they can see pioneer artifacts and perhaps even see a demonstration of some of the cooking, farming, or building techniques used in the period.

Time

This topic deals with keeping time, telling time, and tracking events in time. The concept of time is one that develops within the primary division when students learn to differentiate between past, present, and future. Technological developments are responsible for the modern day emphasis on the importance of time. Technology has changed the way humans consider time from the rotation of the sun through the sky to the ticking of microseconds in a computer chip. Through activities with technology, students are able to understand the concept of time and timing.

The activities that follow challenge students to develop devices that tell time, keep track of time with music, and compare timing of separate events. They help students to predict events based on past performance, to see changes over time in themselves and their families, and to investigate time long past with models of dinosaurs. These activities are time well spent.

Family & Friends

The family and friends theme allows primary students to relate personal experience with their family to relationships beyond the family. Technology in and around the home is part of the family experience. This unit can become the springboard for science, mathematics, and language arts activities.

The home abounds with technological problem solving opportunities. In the activities within this theme, students think about some of the problems that can occur around the home and consider solutions to them. The class could have an excellent opportunity to explore the technology of cooking as they recreate the story *Stone Soup* in the classroom. They will explore the tools, materials, and processes used in household cleaning and maintenance chores through activities at school and at home. They will consider communications problems and solutions as they attempt to find ways to keep the family ties together over long distances. They will also attempt to find ways to keep the family peace by developing a game that can be used to entertain children on vacation. They will design solutions to the inevitable clutter that develops on desk tops and counters around the home and attempt to design an alarm system to ward off unwanted visitors.

UNIT 1

Communities

Activities:

1A: OUR TOWN

1B: CROSSING GUARD

1C: HUFFIN' & PUFFIN'

1D: COMMUNICATOR

1E: SECOND TIME AROUND

1F: PUDDLE PLAY

1G: FAIR PLAY

ACTIVITY 1A:

Our Town

For Your Interest

Town planners, engineers, and architects create models of their plans to present their visions to the politicians and public. These three dimensional presentations are more easily understood than two-dimensional floor plans, elevations, and site plans. They often include details such as bushes, trees, and people.

Many lay people have difficulty interpreting road maps or floor layouts such as those shopping malls. Two dimensional representations of the three dimensional world requires the use of symbols and leaves a lot to the viewer's imagination. Three dimensional models, on the other hand, are simply miniature versions of reality. With models that are made to scale, where all dimensions are in proportion to the real world, the scenes appears to be an actual view of the planned structures viewed from some distance.

NEED

(what are we being asked to do?)

To make a detailed map of our community so that:

We can see all the roads, buildings, trees, and signs.

OR We can show visitors where things are and how to get around.

OTHER "IDEAS" OR "QUESTIONS" WE COULD THINK ABOUT

- *How will we know where everything should go?*

For example:
- walk around the community and make a plan?
- take photographs or draw pictures of important locations around the community?
- use a street map of the community?
- ?

IDEAS

(what ideas do we have for doing it?)

- **What will the detailed map of our community show?**

For example:
- streets?
- buildings (houses, apartments, stores, schools, churches, etc.)?
- trees, streams, rivers, ponds, etc.?
- street signs, stop lights, bus shelters, bridges, etc.?
- parks and playgrounds?
- ?

- **Are there other things we want on the map?**

For example:
- electricity lines?
- fire hydrants?
- phone booths?
- playground equipment?
- street lights?
- ?

CREATE
(how can we make it?)

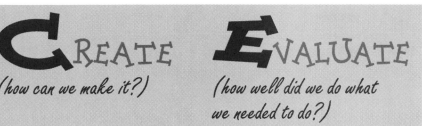

- **What materials are we going to use?**

  For example:
  - mural paper, Bristol board or plywood for a "base"?
  - twigs or pipe cleaners for trees and bushes?
  - small boxes, cardboard, blocks, or wood structures for buildings?
  - barbecue skewers or stir sticks for signs and lamp posts?
  - paint or colored paper for roads, ponds, streams, or rivers?
  - ?

- **What tools and equipment do we need?**

  For example:
  - for measuring?
  - for cutting?
  - for drawing?
  - for attaching?
  - ?

OTHER "IDEAS" OR "QUESTIONS" WE COULD THINK ABOUT

- *How can all the work get done?*

  For example:
  - each student or small groups take charge of small sections of the map?
  - each student or small groups can do one street or one corner?
  - ?

EVALUATE
(how well did we do what we needed to do?)

- **Does the map "work?"**
- **Were all the details we included necessary?**
- **Can we use the map to follow the path we take home from school? to the park? to our best friend's home?**
- **Could we make it better? How?**

Nicer...

Invite students to create a detailed map/model of their school as a community.

Sparking Interest

- Show different types of maps of the community. A transit map will show different features compared to a topographical map or a road map.
- Show plans for a house. If new development is occurring in your community, builders' brochures can be obtained that show artists renditions of the front of the home as well as floor plans.
- Visit your local high school's drafting classes. Architectural drafting students often develop site plans and models for their dream homes or communities.
- Go for a walk around the community. Make a map showing the streets, parks, homes, and businesses.

ACTIVITY 1B:

Crossing Guard

For Your Interest

With the development of transportation technology in this century many technological problems have been created. Some of these problems such as pollution and accident prevention (or damage reduction) have required very sophisticated technological solutions. Engine and fuel improvements, emission control devices, seat belts, air bags, and anti-lock braking systems have all been invented to satisfy needs created by the automobile.

Some of the problems have been solved with much simpler solutions. The problem of pedestrians crossing a busy street is a technological problem. The solutions range from cross walks, bridges, and underpasses through crossing guards and traffic cops, to traffic lights which may be computer-controlled.

Need
(what are we being asked to do?)

To invent a set of rules and signals for directing traffic so that:

We can role play what happens when we cross a busy street.

OR We can practice road safety at school.

Ideas
(what ideas do we have for doing it?)

- **What different types of traffic are there at street crossings?**

  For example:
  - cars?
  - bicycles?
  - people?
  - pets?
  - baby carriages?
  - ?

- **How do crossing guards direct all this traffic?**

  For example:
  - hand held signs?
  - hand signals?
  - whistles?
  - flashlights?
  - ?

- **Are the rules the same for all the traffic?**

  For example:
  - do bicycles follow the rules that cars do?
  - do skate boarders follow the same rules that cars do?

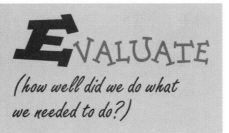

Create
(how can we make it?)

- How will we let the different types of traffic know what it can do and when it can do it?

  For example:
  – hand signs
  – colored lights?
  – a stop/go sign?
  – ?

- How are we going to be noticed by the drivers and pedestrians in all kinds of weather?

  For example:
  – will we have signs?
  – will we have bright uniforms?
  – will we carry flashlights?
  – ?

Evaluate
(how well did we do what we needed to do?)

- How will we test our system?
- Did our rules and signals work?
- Could we make them better? How?

Nicer...

Invite students to create a system of corridor traffic control in their school.

Sparking Interest

- Invite a police officer, crossing guard, or school bus driver into the class to discuss pedestrian road safety.
- Collect posters or pictures which promote pedestrian road safety.
- Tell or read a story which involves children and traffic safety.

ACTIVITY 1C:

Huffin' and Puffin'

For Your Interest

A wide variety of materials are used to build structures or shelters. The choice of materials is determined to a large extent by location, climate and technology available. In a cold climate the structure needs to be able to keep in the heat and keep out the cold winds and snow. In hot climates it is more important to provide shelter from the sun and wind. Rain may be a concern in some areas. Insects or other forms of wildlife may have to be considered in other areas.

The technology available determines what materials can be used effectively and economically. Bricks can be made of snow in the arctic or of mud and straw in the tropical climates. Tents can be made from animal skins or cotton depending on the available resources and the ability (technology) to fashion the raw materials into sheets. Wood may be used in some areas but its cost (abundance and technology) determines whether rude logs or milled lumber will be used as the building material.

Need (what are we being asked to do?)

To build a model house that can stand the "huff and puff" of the wolf so that:

We can learn about strong structures.

OR We can investigate different ways to build structures.

OR We can tell the pigs what kind of house to build.

Ideas (what ideas do we have for doing it?)

- **What materials can we use to build the house?**

For example:
- newspaper?
- drinking straws?
- popsicle sticks?
- sugar cubes?
- ?

- **What can we use to hold or join the materials together?**

For example:
- bend or fold the materials?
- stack or overlap the materials?
- glue or tape the material?
- staple or nail the material?
- ?

- **How will we design our model house?**

For example:
- tall and thin?
- short and fat?
- round or dome shaped?
- square or rectangular shapes?
- triangular or pyramid shaped?
- ?

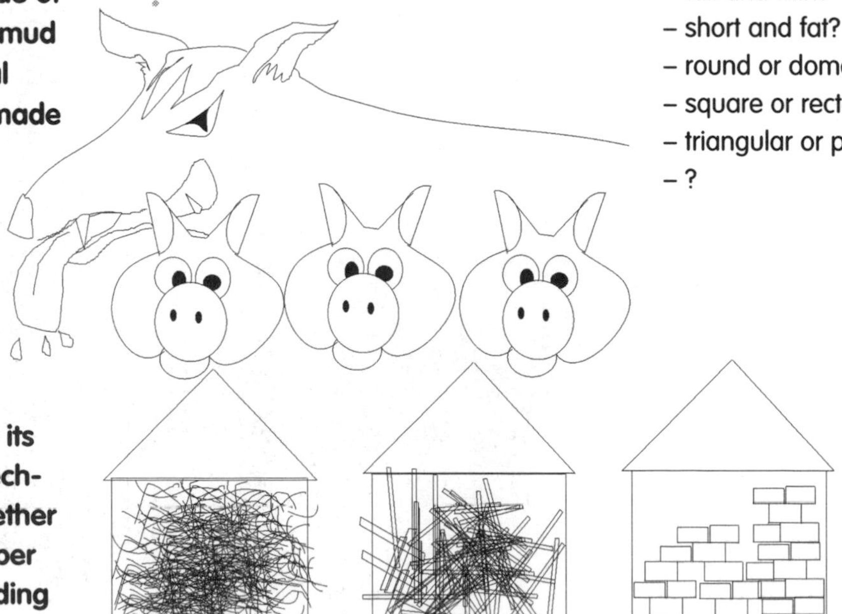

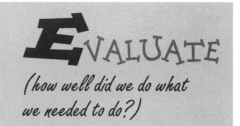

Create
(how can we make it?)

- **What material do we want to use?**

  For example:
  - paper?
  - straws?
  - wood?
  - ?

- **What tools and equipment do we need?**

  For example:
  - scissors?
  - saws?
  - glue?
  - tape?
  - ?

- **What can we use to test the strength of the house?**

  For example:
  - a house fan?
  - a hairdryer?
  - ?

- **How can we make sure the test is fair?**

  For example:
  - is the distance between the house and the fan the same for each test?
  - is the fan set to the same force (speed) for each test?
  - is the time that the fan is on the same for each test?

Evaluate
(how well did we do what we needed to do?)

- **Which model house stayed up or stayed in place the longest?**
- **What makes the houses strong (materials? fasteners? shape? quality of construction?)?**
- **Could we make our house better? How?**

Nicer...

In some communities, earthquakes are a greater threat than tornadoes and hurricanes. Invite students to design earthquake-proof houses and test them by shaking or tilting the desk on which they are built.

Sparking Interest

- Read the story of the Three Little Pigs.
- Compare different forms of shelter used by people around the world.
- Collect pictures of houses.
- Read a book or tell a story about building a house.
- Collect information (pictures) about storms and the damage that can be done by wind during hurricanes and tornadoes.

▶ Communities

ACTIVITY 1D:

Communicator

For Your Interest

In the past, students could publicize their classroom activities through such media as student-designed newspapers, posters and flyers—in other words, through print and paper-dependent means. Today, computer-mediated methods of communications (e-mail, the NET, electronic publishing, teleconferencing) have greatly expanded the options available.

NEED

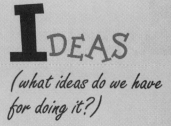

(what are we being asked to do?)

To communicate news and information about class events so that:

We can let other classes know what we are doing.

OR We can inform parents about what we're doing.

IDEAS

(what ideas do we have for doing it?)

- **What kinds of classroom news and information do we want other people to know about?**

  For example:
  - parents' night?
  - class play?
  - fund–raisers?
  - ?

- **What ways are there to communicate classroom news and information?**

  For example:
  - newspaper?
  - poster?
  - newsletter?
  - radio?
  - e-mail?
  - web site?
  - ?

- **What skills are needed for each of these ways?**

  For example:
  - gathering information (names, locations, dates, times, results, scores, etc.)?
  - organizing and presenting the information?
  - writing and editing text?
  - creating catchy titles or headlines?
  - developing and/or using visual materials such as colors schemes and graphics?
  - keying in or printing text copy?
  - ?

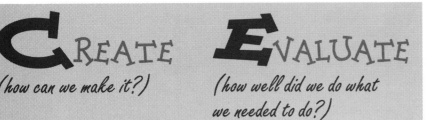

CREATE
(how can we make it?)

- What materials do we need?
  - (Answers will depend on the medium chosen for the messages.)
- What tools and equipment do we need?
  - (Answers will depend on the medium chosen for the messages.)

EVALUATE
(how well did we do what we needed to do?)

- What did people like about our communication? Was there anything they didn't like?
- What could we do differently?

Nicer...

Invite the class to submit a design for the school's website home page.

Sparking Interest

News used to be shared with the public only through official or government agencies. As early as 59 BC, news in Rome of social and political events was carried in a daily gazette called Acta Diurna (Daily Events). This publication was posted in public places. (This method of spreading the news was also used in China during the cultural revolution in the 20th century, as well as in many other places.) In the middle ages books and pamphlets were circulated which kept the few citizens who could read in touch with major events. With the invention of the printing press and the increase of literacy in the middle classes, newspapers began to be published in port cities. News was carried by ships' captains.

Today the news is carried by electronic as well as print media. Television, radio, and the internet provide the public with a variety of views of the news. Popular news shows focus on sporting events and the entertainment industry. Business and political news is available every hour of the day. Even the weather has its own news station.

ACTIVITY 1E:

Second Time Around

For Your Interest

In the past, when resources were more scarce, people wasted little. They reused and repaired things that they owned because replacing them was an expensive option.

Technology has increased our access to resources and we, thus, tend to have less regard for material things than our grandparents did. We waste resources because they are cheap, and we've had the luxury of becoming lazy about reusing. Technology will not be able to maintain indefinitely the supply of resources that we require for this lifestyle. In the long run, or perhaps not-so-long run, the finite nature of our world's resources will change the economics of the throwaway society. For young children, of course, we need to help them feel they can make a difference, helping to ensure we have a good environment in which to live in the future, hence this activity.

NEED

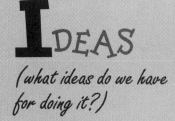

(what are we being asked to do?)

To recover parts from discarded items so that:

We can sort them and save them for other uses.
OR We can prevent waste.
OR We can help protect the environment.

IDEAS

(what ideas do we have for doing it?)

- **What kinds of items do people throw away?**

For example:
- old or broken toys?
- old containers?
- old or broken appliances?
- ?

- **What parts of these can be reused?**

For example:
- dials, knobs and lamps?
- bolts, nuts, screws, and washers?
- gears, levers, springs, pulleys, and cables?
- ?

- **How can we reuse them?**

For example:
- to make new things?
- to fix items that are broken?
- as decoration in art projects (mobiles, mosaics, etc.)?
- ?

- **What can we do with the leftover parts that we can't use?**

For example:
- recycle them through your local waste management system?
- turn them into junk sculpture?
- take them to a junk yard?
- ?

CREATE
(how can we make it?)

- **What tools and equipment do we need to take them apart SAFELY?**

  For example:
  - safety glasses?
  - cutting and gripping pliers?
  - assorted screwdrivers?
  - small socket driver set?
  - ?

- **How can we sort the parts?**

  For example:
  - by colour?
  - by size?
  - by shape?
  - by type?
  - ?

- **How can we store them?**

  For example:
  - plastic food containers?
  - shoe boxes?
  - egg cartons?
  - ?

EVALUATE
(how well did we do what we needed to do?)

- **Did we recover all the parts we wanted?**
- **Did we recover any parts we didn't expect to find?**
- **Were there some parts we couldn't recover? Why?**
- **How well can we use the tools? Which tools were easier to use?**
- **Could we make our way of sorting and storing the parts better? How?**

Nicer...

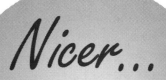

Invite the students to name the parts that they have recovered. Catalogues from an electronics supplier and a fasteners supplier could be used as references, or students could invent their own names.

Sparking Interest

- Discuss the three "Rs"—Reduce, Reuse, Recycle.
- Display posters which promote waste reduction.

ACTIVITY 1F:

Puddle Play

For Your Interest

A puddle in the school yard invites splashing, wading, and creativity. This activity builds on children's natural attraction to water. If the school yard is dry, use a hula hoop with a large plastic garbage bag laid over it to make your own puddle. Whether the puddle is natural or teacher-created, the students will enjoy the opportunity to experiment and play with puddle boats.

Making boats is more than just creating things that float. The challenge that follows requires students to consider different ways of powering their boats. They will need a source of energy. The wind can be used through sails. Elastic bands can be wound up and released to power propellers or paddle wheels. Batteries or solar cells may be used to drive electric motors. A balloon may be inflated to provide "jet" power. Children should be encouraged to experiment with different energy sources prior to designing their boats.

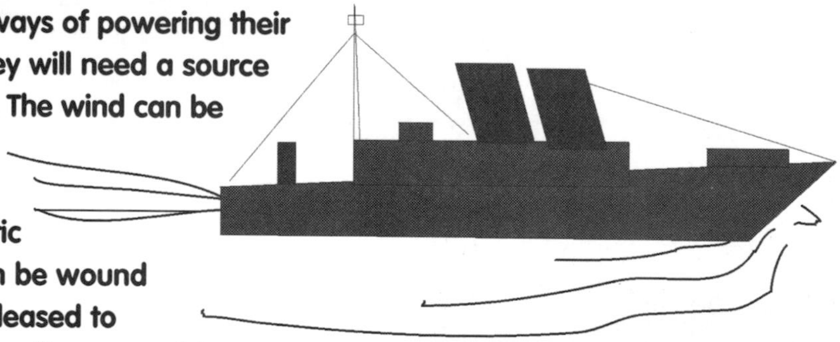

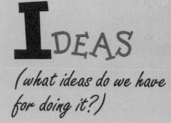

NEED
(what are we being asked to do?)

To make a powered puddle boat so that:

We can experiment with different ways to make it go.

OR We can see how fast we can make it go.

OR We can see how far we can make it go.

IDEAS
(what ideas do we have for doing it?)

- **What materials can we use that will float on water?**

For example:
– wood?
– plastic?
– foil?
– cardboard?
– paper?
– ?

- **What shape will our puddle boat be?**

For example:
– like a raft?
– like a row boat or canoe?
– like a ship?
– ?

- **How will we power the puddle boat?**

For example:
– human power (push it)?
– air power?
– wind power?
– battery power?
– elastic power?
– ?

- **What will help make the boat move?**

– a sail?
– a propeller?
– a paddle wheel?
– ?

CREATE
(how can we make it?)

- **What materials do we want to use?**
  - (Answers will depend on design choices students make.)
- **What tools and equipment do we need?**
  - (Answers will depend on design choices students make.)
- **What can we do if our ideas don't work?**

  For example:
  - talk with other students to see what they're doing?
  - try other ideas?
  - ?

EVALUATE
(how well did we do what we needed to do?)

- **How well did our puddle boat work? (How far did it go? How fast did it go? Did it go straight?)**
- **How were other boats in our class the same? How were they different?**
- **Could we make our boat better? How?**

Nicer...

Invite students to design suitable footwear for playing in puddles, perhaps to keep their feet warm and dry while they test their puddle boats.

Sparking Interest

- Read or tell a story about toy boats.
- Collect and display bathtub and other toy boats.

ACTIVITY 1G:

Fair Play

For Your Interest

In rural towns and cities, the county fair or fall agricultural fair is an institution in which harvests are celebrated and families join with communities to have fun. The amusement park which frequently accompanies the fairs are enjoyed by young and old alike. Besides traditional rides like the merry-go-round there are games of skill like ring toss and similar fixed- and moving-target games where participants attempt to win prizes by completing apparently simple tasks.

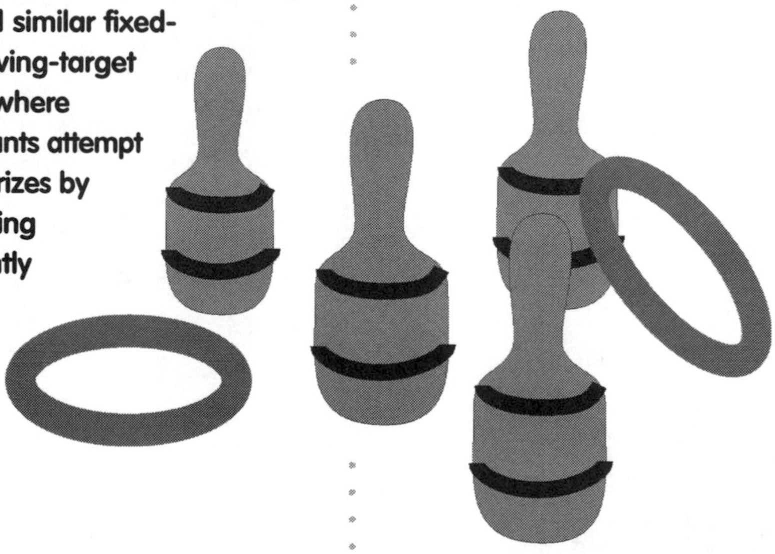

Need (what are we being asked to do?)

To design a game of skill so that:

We can have a classroom arcade.

OR We can have a fund-raiser fun-fare.

Ideas (what ideas do we have for doing it?)

- **What kind of game will we invent?**

For example:
- ring toss?
- mini golf?
- bowling?
- bean bag toss?
- ?

- **What materials could we use?**

For example:
- bean bags?
- Frisbees?
- balls?
- blocks?
- juice bottles, pop cans, etc.?
- ?

Sparking Interest:

- Discuss games that require skill, like bull's-eye games.
- Ask students who have been to country or agricultural fairs to describe what they saw and what they did.

CREATE
(how can we make it?)

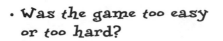

- **What materials will we use?**
  - (This will depend on the type of game that the students choose to make. They need to think about making the game attractive as well as functional.)
- **What tools and equipment do we need?**

  For example:
  - ruler?
  - marker/crayon/paint?
  - pencil?
  - scissors?
  - tape?
  - ?
- **How can we make sure that everyone knows the rules?**

  For example:
  - explain them as they begin the game?
  - write them out on a poster?
  - draw pictures showing the way they are supposed to play?
  - ?

EVALUATE
(how well did we do what we needed to do?)

- **Was the game too easy or too hard?**
- **Did everyone enjoy the game?**
- **Did everyone know how to play properly?**
- **Could we improve it? How?**

OTHER "IDEAS" OR "QUESTIONS" WE COULD THINK ABOUT

- What will we call our game?
- Do we want to make a sign with the name of our game?
- Do we need prizes for people who win?

Nicer...

Invite the students to open their amusement park to other classes. They could charge (dimes or quarters) to the students to raise money for classroom field trips or other school activities.

UNIT 2

Story Time

Activities:

2A: THE PIED PIPER

2B: KING ARTHUR'S COURT

2C: STORYLAND PAGEANT

2D: JACK & THE GIANT

2E: A TOWERING CHALLENGE

2F: BEAR WITH ME

2G: COLLECTIBLES

▶ Story Time

ACTIVITY 2A:

The Pied Piper

For Your Interest

Pipes are an ancient musical invention, and have a strong association with mesmerism and magic. (Think of the pipes played by the Greek god of forests and shepherds, Pan, or the magic flute in Mozart's opera of the same name.) As for the "Pied" portion of the Pied Piper's name, it refers to his two-colour outfit (although the colours are not specifically identified). It's possible that the emphasis on two-ness is intended to symbolize or thematize the piper's dual role in the story as saviour and destroyer.

Sparking Interest

- Read, listen to a recording, or view a video of the story.
- Look at pictures of different kinds of pipes such as penny whistle, flute, recorder, pan pipes, or bag pipes.
- Listen to the different sounds (live or recorded) made by pipes.

NEED

(what are we being asked to do?)

To make a pipe for the Pied Piper so that:

We can help out in case the Piper's pipe breaks.
OR We can role-play the story.
OR We can learn more about musical instruments.

IDEAS

(what ideas do we have for doing it?)

- **What things can we use to make pipe like sounds when we blow?**

  For example:
  - bottles?
  - balloons?
  - drinking straws?
  - hollow tubes of plastic or bamboo?
  - ?

- **How can we make our pipe play different notes?**

  For example:
  - use different pipes for each note?
  - put holes in it to be fingered?
  - move our mouths to make different notes?
  - blow into it with different amounts of force?
  - ?

CREATE
(how can we make it?)

- What materials can we use to make the pipe?

  For example:
  - plastic bottles?
  - narrow tubes?
  - drinking straws?
  - balloons?
  - ?

- What tools or equipment do we need?

  For example:
  - scissors?
  - saws?
  - tape or glue?
  - drills?
  - ?

EVALUATE
(how well did we do what we needed to do?)

- How well does the pipe work?
- Does it play the way we wanted it to?
- How is it different from other pipes made in our class? How is it the same?
- Could we make our pipe better? How?

OTHER "IDEAS" OR "QUESTIONS" WE COULD THINK ABOUT

- What type of pipe would we like to make for the Piper?
- Will the piper be able to carry it easily as he leads the rats out of town?
- How many notes do we want it to play?

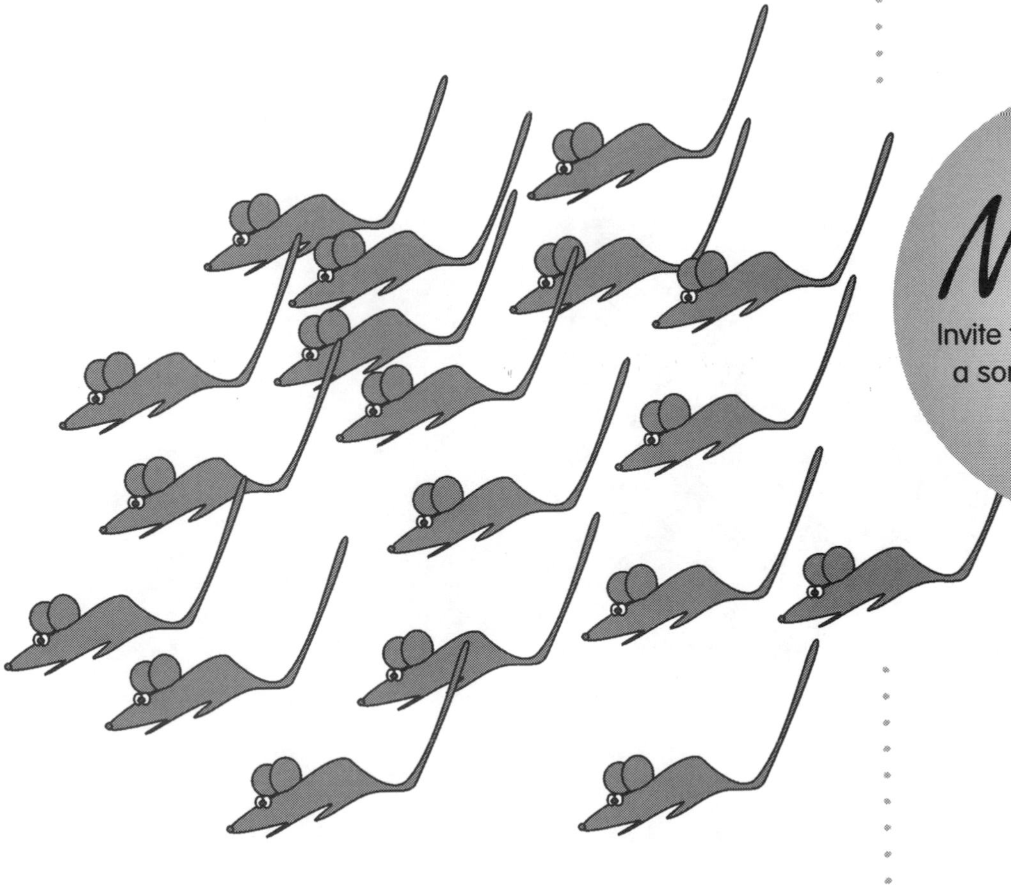

Nicer. . .

Invite the students to perform a song as a group on their instruments.

ACTIVITY 2B:

King Arthur's Court

For Your Interest

The romantic story of Arthur, the Knights of the Round Table, and Camelot has some basis in history. Reality, however, does not centre on shining knights in armour steeped in heraldry and chivalry. The real Arthur was probably a sixth-century Welsh commander who led a successful campaign against the Saxons. During this period of "British history, few battles were fought on horseback and the warriors wore more leather than iron for armour. Arthur may have been a great leader because of his knowledge and use of Roman military practice. He was one of the last successful military leaders of the Britons and stayed in the memory of the Welsh for that reason alone. Oral traditions, being open to embellishment and frequently used to support political and religious motives, modified Arthur's story to rally the people of Wales (and eventually Britain) around a hero of epic proportions.

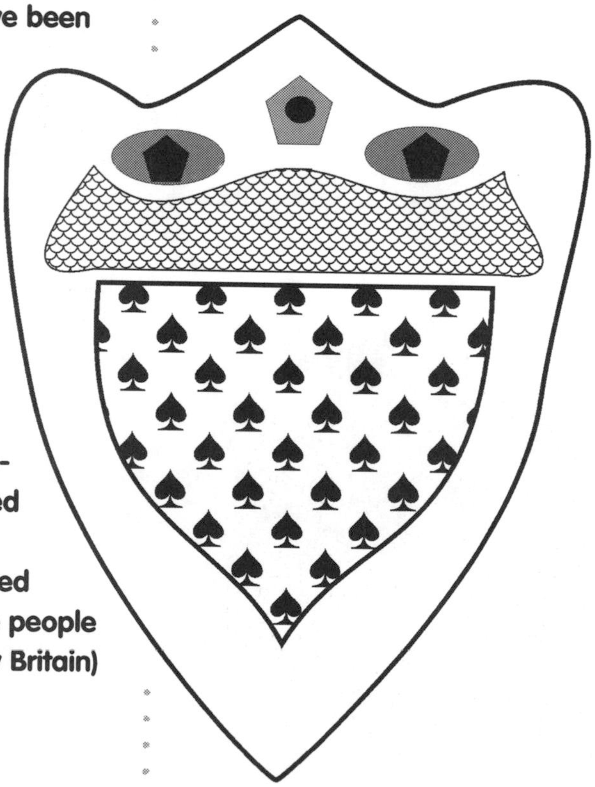

NEED

(what are we being asked to do?)

To make a castle entrance in the classroom so that:

We can have a door to our "enchanted classroom."

OR We can set the mood for a medieval feast.

OR We can role-play in our study of medieval times.

IDEAS

(what ideas do we have for doing it?)

- **What kind of door could the castle entrance have?**

  For example:
  - drawbridge?
  - curtains?
  - portcullis?
  - double door?
  - ?

- **How could the door be opened?**

  For example:
  - pull door handles?
  - raised or lowered with a crank?
  - ?

- **How will the door be held in place?**

  For example:
  - build it into a wall?
  - hold it between some chairs?
  - attach its frame to the ceiling?
  - mount it in the classroom door frame?
  - ?

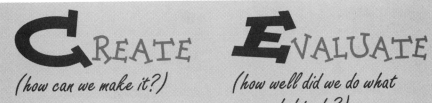

CREATE
(how can we make it?)

- **What materials can we use to make the door?**

  For example:
  - cardboard sheets?
  - cardboard boxes?
  - wood frames and construction paper?
  - rope or string?
  - paint?
  - ?

- **What tools or equipment do we need?**

  For example:
  - scissors?
  - saws?
  - tape or glue?
  - paint and brushes?
  - ?

- **What should we make the door look like?**

  For example:
  - wood?
  - metal?
  - old?
  - new?
  - ?

EVALUATE
(how well did we do what we needed to do?)

- **Does our door work as we expected it to?**
- **Does it look like a castle door?**
- **Could we make it better? How?**

Sparking Interest

- Read or tell some stories from the Arthurian legends.
- Show pictures of knights and castles.
- Visit a museum to look at a medieval display.

OTHER "IDEAS" OR "QUESTIONS" WE COULD THINK ABOUT

- How big does the entrance have to be?
- Do we want to include a window?

Nicer...

Invite the students to decorate the whole classroom like a castle. They could dress up as jesters, jugglers, knights, etc. and perform at a medieval feast, for example.

ACTIVITY 2C:

Storyland Pageant

For Your Interest

Every child has a favourite story, whether it's a novel such as The Wizard of Oz or The Lion, the Witch, and the Wardrobe, a retelling such as The Name of the Tree, or a tale from Dr. Seuss or Robert Munsch. For this activity, individual students are asked to design a mask representing a favourite character from a fairy story. While this outcome may be viewed as an end in itself, spin-off possibilities—such as incorporating all the characters in a play—are varied and rich.

NEED
(what are we being asked to do?)

To make a mask of a character from a favourite story so that:

We can play the role of the character while we tell the story.

OR We can show others what the character looks like.

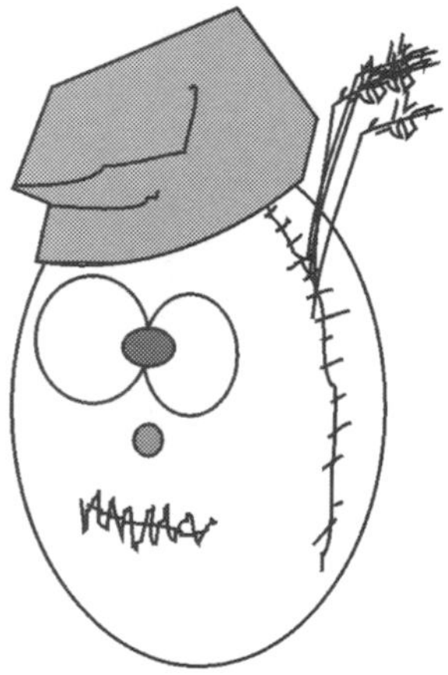

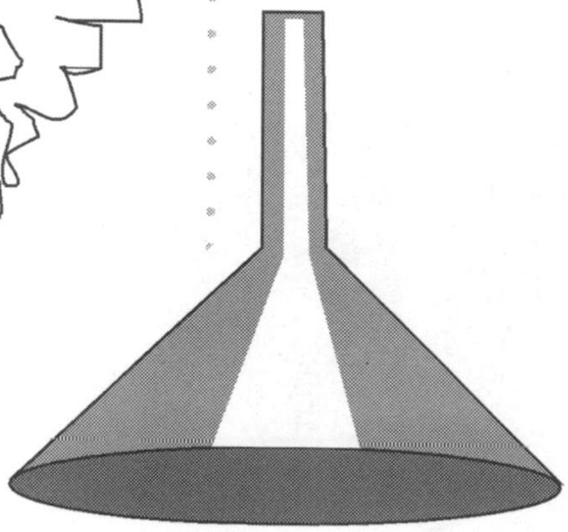

IDEAS
(what ideas do we have for doing it?)

- **What materials can we use to make our mask?**

  For example:
  - paper bag?
  - papier maché?
  - recycled Halloween mask?
  - cereal box?
  - ?

- **How can we see and talk with our mask on?**

  For example:
  - cut holes for eyes and mouth?
  - put mesh over the openings?
  - ?

- **How can we keep our mask on our face or head?**

  For example:
  - use an elastic band?
  - pipe cleaners?
  - string?
  - use arms from old sunglasses?
  - ?

Create
(how can we make it?)

- **What materials do we need to make our mask?**

  For example:
  - newspaper, construction paper, paper bags, fabric?
  - string, yarn, elastics?
  - paint, crayons, markers?
  - ?

- **What do we need to do to make it look like our character?**

  For example:
  - draw, paint or attach features?
  - glue or tape on hair (yarn) or a hat?
  - ?

- **What tools and equipment do we need?**

  For example:
  - scissors?
  - tape?
  - glue?
  - ?

Evaluate
(how well did we do what we needed to do?)

- **Is our mask comfortable when we wear it?**
- **Can we see and speak easily when it's on?**
- **Does it look like the character we want it to be?**
- **Could we make our mask better? How?**

Nicer....

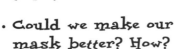

Invite the students to make up plays in small groups with the different characters from their stories. The class could entertain parents or other classes with their dramas.

Sparking Interest

- Ask the class to bring in or tell their favourite stories.
- Show a variety of illustrations of the characters.
- View videos of some stories. (Compare animated versions with those using actors for the parts.)

▶ Story Time

ACTIVITY 2D:

Jack & the Giant

For Your Interest

In the story of Jack and the Beanstalk, the hero steals from the giant and kills him to escape with the loot. Such antisocial behaviour is justified by virtue of the underlying context of the tale. Giants are a part of the story traditions of many cultures, and often abuse or kill humans, seemingly for sport. They're the stereotypical "bad guys." A hero (one of the "good guys") must overcome superior strength or power to defeat them, and anything—even robbery and murder—is considered appropriate. Contemporary analogies often include large corporations, wealthy entrepreneurs, or powerful politicians being defeated by righteous, but relatively ordinary, citizens—although we tend to frown on the murder part, except in the movies.

NEED

(what are we being asked to do?)

To design a way for Jack to escape so that:

We can help him get away from the giant quickly.

OR We can get Jack back home safely before the giant can get there.

IDEAS

(what ideas do we have for doing it?)

- **What ways can Jack get to the ground from up in the giant's house?**

  For example:
  - climb?
  - slide?
  - jump?
  - float?
  - ride?
  - ?

- **What can Jack use to make sure he gets down safely?**

  For example:
  - rope?
  - parachute?
  - airplane?
  - ladder?
  - bungie cord?
  - elevator?
  - ?

- **What "giant-size" materials can Jack use to design and make his escape?**

  For example:
  - plant leaves for wings, a parachute, or a slide?
  - vines for a rope or a bungie cord?
  - flower petals for a parachute?
  - ?

- **How will we test our escape plan to see if it works and is safe?**

  For example:
  - use a small toy figurine to test it off a table?
  - use an egg to test it off a table?
  - ?

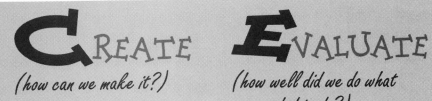

Create
(how can we make it?)

- **What materials can we use to help Jack?**

  For example:
  - – construction paper?
  - – string?
  - – elastics?
  - – drinking straws?
  - – wood?
  - – ?

- **What tools and equipment do we need?**

  For example:
  - – tape or glue?
  - – saw?
  - – scissors
  - – ?

Evaluate
(how well did we do what we needed to do?)

- **Does our escape plan work well?**
- **Would the giant be able to use it too?**
- **Can we make the escape plan work better? How?**

Nicer...

Increase (or decrease) the mass (or size, or both) of the "Jack" model to investigate how the escape plan might have to change.

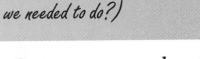

Sparking Interest

- Read or tell the story.
- Show a video of the story.
- Grow some beans in the classroom.

▶ Story Time

ACTIVITY 2E:

A Towering Challenge

For Your Interest

Towers are a powerful symbol of human engineering and ingenuity. For millennia, towers have been erected to glorify (or sometimes to challenge) the supremacy of a higher authority. This tradition continues even today, with the office towers of corporations dominating the skylines of major cities around the world, symbolizing their power and economic status. Likewise, cities—from Paris to St. Louis to Toronto—find reasons to erect towers in their own honour. But at a more practical level, a key function of towers is to raise us (or our technology) above the ground so we can, for example, trail electrical wires across the landscape, erect storage tanks for water, or simply bring us eye-to-eye with something or (as in this activity) someone.

NEED

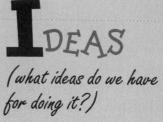

(what are we being asked to do?)

To build a tower as tall as possible so that:

We can help the Lilliputians talk with Gulliver face-to-face.

IDEAS

(what ideas do we have for doing it?)

- **What shapes are tall towers?**

  For example:
  – rectangles (like apartment buildings)?
  – triangles (like pyramids)
  – cylinders (like the Tower of Pisa)?
  – ?

- **What materials are used to build real towers?**

  For example:
  – concrete?
  – steel beams?
  – stone or cement block?
  – wires?
  – ?

- **What keeps real towers from falling over?**

  For example:
  – shape (wider at bottom)?
  – base buried in ground?
  – wires?
  – ?

- **How can we fasten our tower to the ground?**

  For example:
  – glue it to a base?
  – tape it to the floor?
  – bury it in sand?
  – ?

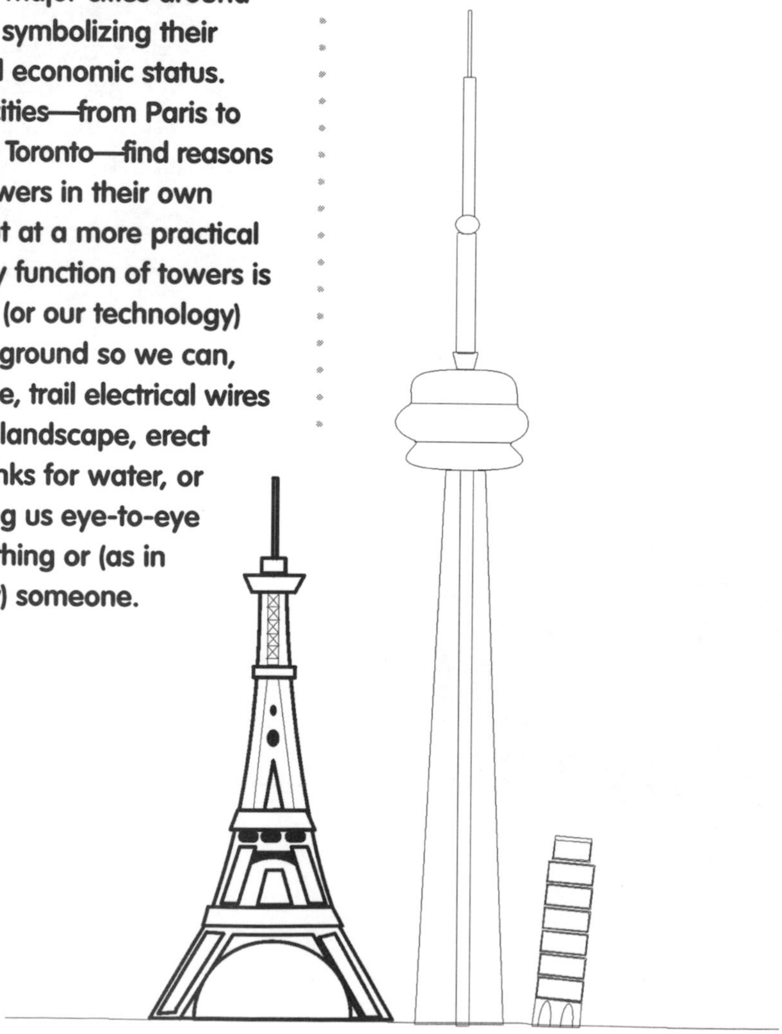

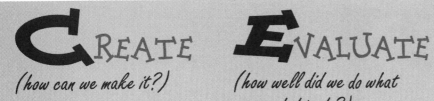

CREATE
(how can we make it?)

- What materials are in the classroom that we can use to build our tower?

  For example:
  - found material?
  - construction kits?
  - straws, paper, toothpicks, etc.?
  - ?
- What tools and equipment do we need?

  For example:
  - saw?
  - screwdriver?
  - glue?
  - scissors?
  - ?

EVALUATE
(how well did we do what we needed to do?)

- Does our tower stand by itself?
- How steady is it? Will the Lilliputians fall off if it's windy?
- How is our tower like others in the class? How is it different?
- Could we make our tower better? How?

OTHER "IDEAS" OR "QUESTIONS" WE COULD THINK ABOUT

- How will we make our tower steady so the Lilliputians don't fall off?
- How will the Lilliputians get to the top of the tower?
- Do the Lilliputians need a platform to stand on?

Nicer...

Invite the students to build tall towers with limited material, or to design and build earthquake-proof towers. (Simulate earthquakes by shaking the desk or table on which they stand.)

Sparking Interest

Read or tell the story of Gulliver and the Lilliputians.
Collect pictures of different types of towers in and around your community.
Collect or find pictures of world famous towers (CN Tower, Eiffel tower, Empire State Building, Seattle Space Needle, Tower of London)

Story Time

ACTIVITY 2F:

Bear with Me

For Your Interest

When Goldilocks broke into the home of the three bears, she ate their food and broke their furniture. If the tale were set in our modern society, it's quite likely that poor Goldi wouldn't stand a chance. In fact, in this day and age of home security systems, high-tech surveillance techniques, neighbourhood watch programs, growing numbers of street youth, and even entire communities sheltered behind brick walls and security guards, perhaps the story of Goldilocks and the three bears is nearing the end of its tether to the gilded meadows of storytime. On the other hand, maybe it will still be popular with children in the 22nd and 23rd centuries.

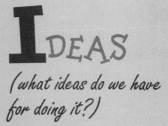

NEED (what are we being asked to do?)	IDEAS (what ideas do we have for doing it?)

To make an alarm system so that:

We can help the bears scare unwanted people out of their house.

- **What things can we use to make alarm noises?**

  For example:
  - bells?
  - chimes?
  - tin cans?
  - rattles?
  - ?

- **What can trigger or start the alarm?**

  For example:
  - string as a trip wire across the doorway?
  - the door itself?
  - an electric switch?
  - a photocell
  - ?

- **How can we test our alarm system?**

  For example:
  - test it on the classroom door?
  - test it on a closet or cupboard door?
  - make a door to test it on?
  - ?

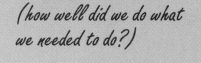

Create
(how can we make it?)

- **What materials do we want to use to make the alarm?**

  For example:
  - marbles and a tin can?
  - bells or chimes?
  - electric bell or buzzer and batteries from an electricity kit?
  - ?

- **What materials do we want to use to make the switch?**

  For example:
  - string?
  - elastic bands?
  - electric switches or push buttons from an electricity kit?
  - ?

- **What tools and equipment do we need?**

  For example:
  - scissors?
  - tape or glue?
  - pliers, wire, etc.?
  - ?

Evaluate
(how well did we do what we needed to do?)

- **Does our alarm work?**
- **Is it loud enough?**
- **How is our alarm different from others in the class? How is it similar?**
- **Could we make our alarm better? How?**

OTHER "IDEAS" OR "QUESTIONS" WE COULD THINK ABOUT

- How loud should the alarm be?
- How long does it have to make noise?
- How can the bears get into their home without setting off the alarm?

Nicer...

Invite students to develop a time delay for their alarm so that, for example, the alarm sounds 30 seconds after the trigger mechanism is activated.

Sparking Interest

- Read the story of Goldilocks and the Three Bears.
- Show the class the timer for the school's bell system.
- Invite the principal or caretaker to describe the intruder alarm system used in the school.
- Discuss places where alarms are used to deter intruders.

Story Time

ACTIVITY 2G:

Collectibles

For Your Interest

When Hollywood film companies and the TV networks produce shows for youngsters, they sometimes attempt to market not only the film and video, but also collectibles related to the story. (Similar techniques are used by some book and comic book publishers.) Money from sales of action figures, clothing, toys, picture books, and cards in many cases exceeds the profits from the box office. Some movies, which are aimed at mature audiences, also reap profits from children who have never seen the film but demand the collectible spin-offs.

Sparking Interest

- Make a display or show pictures of collectibles based on books and movies.
- Ask the students to bring in action figures and dolls based on stories or movie

NEED
(what are we being asked to do?)

To make a set of collectible cards based on our favourite story so that:

We can trade them with other people in the class.

OR We can show others the best parts or characters from a story, TV show, or movie.

We can sell them at a fund-raiser

IDEAS
(what ideas do we have for doing it?)

- **What card collections do we have that are based on stories, TV shows, or movies?**

  For example:
  - Star Wars?
  - Pocahantas?
  - X-Men?
  - Power Rangers?
  - ?

- **What pictures are on the cards?**

  For example:
  - heroes and villains?
  - action scenes?
  - costumes?
  - animals?
  - ?

- **What words are on the cards?**

  For example:
  - the name of the story or movie?
  - the name of the character or event, etc.?
  - a card number?
  - ?

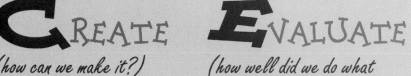

CREATE
(how can we make it?)

- **What stories or movies would we like to base our card collection on?**
- **How will we make pictures for our cards?**

  For example:
  - cut them out from magazines?
  - draw them?
  - use the computer?
  - ?
- **How will we add words to our cards?**

  For example:
  - hand-print them?
  - use the computer?
  - ?
- **What materials and equipment do we need?**

  For example:
  - recyclable paper or cardboard?
  - coloured pencils, crayons, markers?
  - scissors?
  - graphics software?
  - glue or tape?
  - ?

EVALUATE
(how well did we do what we needed to do?)

- **What was the hardest part of making our cards? What was the easiest?**
- **How is our card collection different from others created in our class?**
- **Could we make our card collection better? How?**

OTHER "IDEAS" OR "QUESTIONS" WE COULD THINK ABOUT

- How big are the cards?
- What is on the back of the cards?
- How many cards will we need for a collection?
- Do we want any "Special Edition" card in our collection?

Nicer...

Invite students to design an advertising campaign to market their card collections.

UNIT 3

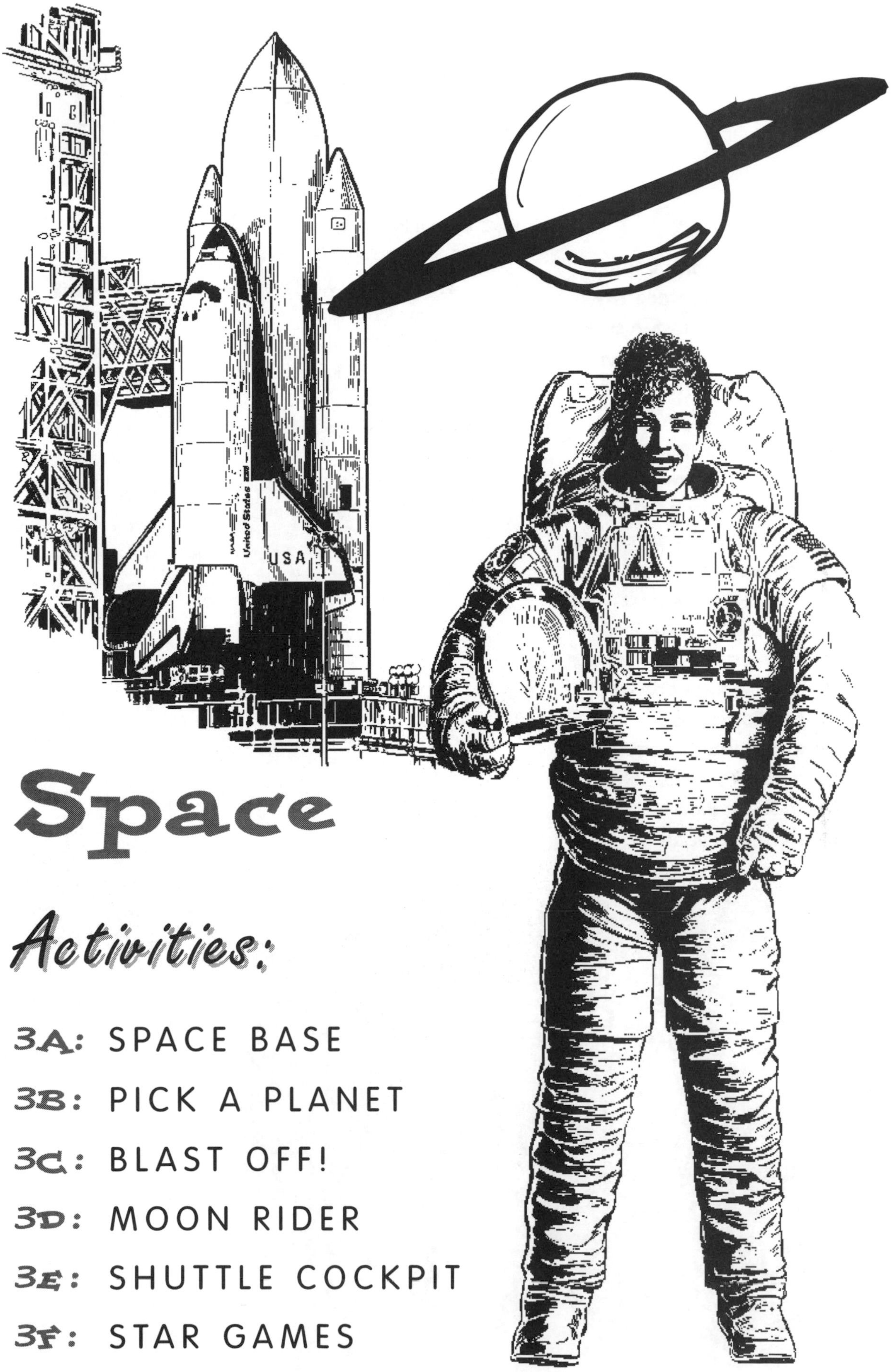

Space

Activities:

3A: SPACE BASE

3B: PICK A PLANET

3C: BLAST OFF!

3D: MOON RIDER

3E: SHUTTLE COCKPIT

3F: STAR GAMES

ACTIVITY 3A:

Space Base

For Your Interest

As astronauts go further into space, they need a place where they can refuel and rest. A space station provides this opportunity. In early 1971, the former Soviet Union launched Salyut 1, the world's first space station. Since then, a number of newer models of the Salyut design have been launched and used by astronauts. In 1984, a crew of Russian cosmonauts stayed in space aboard the space station Salyut 7 for 237 days. The most recent space station to circle the earth is called MIR. Both Russian and American astronauts visited this space station. One cosmonaut stayed on the station for 326 days, almost one year!

Sparking Interest

- Show pictures of a space station from a magazine, comic book, or TV show.
- There are many movies and TV shows that depict life on space stations of the future. Show a clip from one of them.
- Load a suitable computer program that shows current or futuristic views of space stations.
- Tell or invent a story about a space station.

Display a model or toy space station (for example, Space Lego).

NEED
(what are we being asked to do?)

To make a model of a space station so that:

We can show what a space station looks like.

OR We can demonstrate the activities that take place on a space station.

OR We can have a toy to play with.

OR We can decorate the classroom for our space unit.

IDEAS
(what ideas do we have for doing it?)

- **What will it look like on the outside?**

For example:
- shape?
- colour?
- doors?
- places for space ships to land?
- size?
- windows?
- markings?
- ?

- **What will it look like on the inside?**

For example:
- how many rooms?
- what kinds of rooms?
- what furniture?
- what equipment?
- ?

- **What does the space station need for people to live and work there?**

For example:
- how will they breathe?
- where will they get their food?
- where will they sleep?
- how will they keep warm or cool?
- where will supplies and equipment be stored?
- how will people get from place to place in the station?
- ?

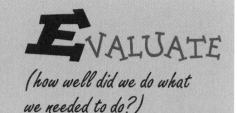

CREATE
(how can we make it?)

- **What materials would be good for building the space station?**

  For example:
  - wood?
  - cardboard?
  - paper?
  - plastic?
- **What tools and equipment do we need or want?**

  For example:
  - construction kits?
  - metal-coloured paints?
  - papier maché?

EVALUATE
(how well did we do what we needed to do?)

- **Did we do everything that we planned? (if not, why did we change our mind?)**
- **What do other space stations in the class look like? How are they different?**
- **Could we make our model better? How?**

OTHER "IDEAS" OR "QUESTIONS" WE COULD THINK ABOUT

- Will the station have moving parts? What parts will move? How can they be made to move?
- Does the station need protection from meteors or invaders?
- ?

Nicer...

Challenge students to outfit their model (or a new one) with a working "space arm." It should be able to move in different directions, grab and hold objects, and fold up for easy storage. Also consider having students "launch" their stations into cyberspace so other classes can visit or comment.

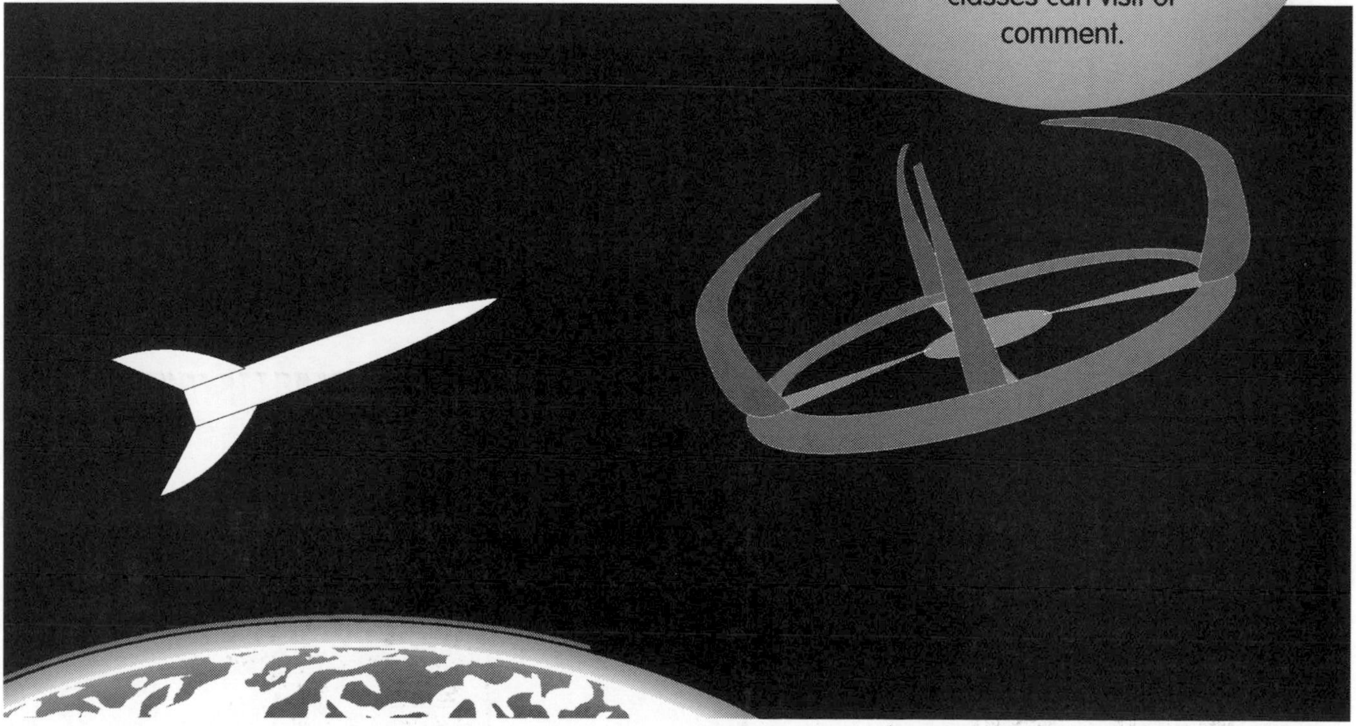

ACTIVITY 3B:

Pick a Planet

By 1990, robotic probes had visited every planet, and many moons, of our solar system, except for Pluto. (In 1996, the Hubble telescope provided our first "close-up" view of that last of our planetary siblings.) In the waning years of the 20th century, Hubble confirmed decades-long speculation that planets exist elsewhere in our galaxy, and the Galileo probe to Jupiter began a long-term study of our largest planet. Meanwhile, despite several failed missions to the moons of Mars, we've been gearing up for renewed investigation of Mars (an orbiter probe, as well as a surface exploration vehicle) and Saturn (the Cassini probe).

Sparking Interest

- Show pictures of the planets from books and magazines.
- Load a suitable computer program that shows our solar system.
- Display a model or poster of the solar system.

Need

(what are we being asked to do?)

To make models of the planets because:

We want to picture how the solar system looks.

OR We want to decorate the classroom with space-related things.

OR Real models are too expensive to buy or too small.

Ideas

(what ideas do we have for doing it?)

- **Where will the planets be displayed?**

  For example:
  - floor?
  - hang from the ceiling?
  - on the classroom walls?
  - in the school hallway?
  - ?

- **How big will they be?**

  For example:
  - big enough to see them from the front of the room?
  - big enough to see features such as clouds, craters, and rings?
  - big enough to fill up the bulletin board?
  - ?

- **Where can we find information about planets if we need it?**

  For example:
  - books?
  - CD-ROM?
  - encyclopedias?
  - Planetarium?
  - the Internet?
  - ?

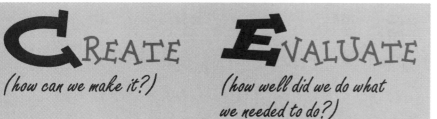

CREATE
(how can we make it?)

- **What materials would we like to use?**

  For example:
  - paper?
  - old, round objects?
  - aluminum foil?
  - balloons?
  - ?

- **What tools and equipment do we need or want?**

  For example:
  - paper plates?
  - balloons and papier maché?
  - paints?
  - ?

EVALUATE
(how well did we do what we needed to do?)

- **Do the models look like real planets?**
- **Are they the right size compared to each other?**
- **Are the models in their proper position in the solar system?**
- **Could we make our planet better? How?**

Nicer...

Invite students to design the planets of an imaginary solar system. Or challenge the students to add moons, the asteroid belt, and perhaps a comet or two to their solar system model.

ACTIVITY 3C:

Blast Off!

Chinese technologists, experts in the use of gunpowder, were making rockets (missiles and fireworks) over 1000 years ago. However, the idea of using a rocket to send a person into space was first described by the French novelist, Savinien Cyrano de Bergerac, in 1657. Modern rocketry works by exploiting Newton's laws of motion, especially the third law: for every action, there is an equal and opposite reaction. The downward thrust produced when rockets burn fuel pushes the rocket upward. This same principle is known to every child who has ever blown up a balloon and let it go.

NEED

(what are we being asked to do?)

To make a model rocket so that:

OR We can experiment with shapes for rockets.

OR We can experiment with different ways to make them move.

OR We can have a toy to play with.

OR We can decorate the classroom for our space unit.

IDEAS

(what ideas do we have for doing it?)

- **What will be the shape of our rocket?**

  For example:
  - like a missile?
  - like a saucer?
  - like a "Wing" fighter from Star Wars?
  - ?

- **What could we use to power our rocket ship?**

  For example:
  - air from a balloon?
  - elastic band?
  - throw it in the air?
  - launch it from a ramp?
  - ?

- **How will we launch the rocket?**

  For example:
  - throw it by hand
  - make a launch tower?
  - make a launch ramp?
  - ?

- **How will we make the rocket fly straight?**

  For example:
  - give it a pointy nose?
  - give it wings and a tail?
  - make a track for it?
  - make it fly on a sting?
  - ?

Create
(how can we make it?)

- **What materials would be good for building our rocket?**

  For example:
  - cardboard tubes?
  - plastic pop bottles
  - construction paper?
  - elastic bands?
  - ?

- **What tools and equipment do we need or want?**

  For example:
  - construction kits?
  - scissors?
  - glue?
  - tape?
  - ?

Evaluate
(how well did we do what we needed to do?)

- **Did our rocket work?**
- **How far did it go?**
- **Could we launch it more than once without breaking it?**
- **How is it different from the other rockets made in our class?**
- **Could we make it better? How?**

Nicer

Invite students to develop a way to launch and land a space capsule softly from their rocket.

Sparking Interest

- Show pictures of rockets from magazines or books.
- Show a clip from one of the many movies and TV shows that have rocket ships in them.
- Load a suitable computer program that describes space exploration and travel.
- Tell or invent a story about a rocket ship.
- Display a model or toy rocket ship. (for example, Space Lego)

ACTIVITY 3D:

Moon Rider

For Your Interest

On July 30, 1971, the astronauts of Apollo 15 used an electrically powered Lunar Roving Vehicle (a "Rover") to transport them across the lunar landscape. (The first lunar Rover, a Russian invention operated remotely from Earth, had collected soil samples from the Moon a year earlier.) In July, 1997, Mars Pathfinder delivered a six wheeled vehicle named Sojourner to the surface of our neighbouring planet, Mars. Like the Russian Rover it was controlled from Earth by remote control. Its task was to photograph the planet and analyze the rocks and soil on the surface. Robotic, remotely controlled probe-vehicles are now considered indispensable to the exploration of Mars, as well as for here on Earth. For example, Rovers are used to study volcanoes, and Rover-like vehicles are employed to examine, capture, or detonate terrorist bombs.

NEED

(what are we being asked to do?)

To make a vehicle that can move around on different surfaces so that:

We can make a model Lunar Rover.

OR We can see which Lunar Rover designs work well.

IDEAS

(what ideas do we have for doing it?)

- **What is the moon's surface like?**

  For example:
  - rough?
  - sandy?
  - lots of craters (holes)?
  - rocky?
  - slippery?
  - hilly?
  - ?

- **What will the Moon vehicle look like?**

  For example:
  - a car?
  - a dune buggy/ATV?
  - an insect?
  - a reptile?
  - ?

- **How many people can ride in it?**

  For example:
  - will they stand or sit?
  - will there be room for equipment?
  - where will the driver sit?
  - what will keep the riders from falling out?
  - ?

- **How will it move?**

  For example:
  - on wheels? (how many?)
  - on tracks?
  - on skis?
  - on legs?
  - on rollers?
  - ?

Create

(how can we make it?)

- **What materials can we use to make the vehicle?**
  - spools and/or bottle and jar lids?
  - paper tubes?
  - soap dish?
  - straws?
  - hollowed–out fruit?
  - ?
- **What tools and equipment do we need or want?**
  - construction kits?
  - tape?
  - glue?
  - scissors
  - wheels?
  - ?

Evaluate

(how well did we do what we needed to do?)

- **Does our vehicle move?**
- **Can it move in different directions?**
- **Does it stay upright, or does it fall over?**
- **How could we make it better?**

OTHER "IDEAS" OR "QUESTIONS" WE COULD THINK ABOUT

- *What can be used to power the vehicle?*

  For example:
  - batteries?
  - elastics?
  - balloons?
  - ?
- *Where can we test it?*

  For example:
  - a sandbox?
  - the playground?
  - an obstacle course?
  - ?

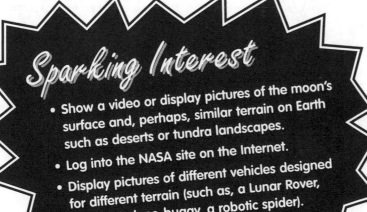

Sparking Interest

- Show a video or display pictures of the moon's surface and, perhaps, similar terrain on Earth such as deserts or tundra landscapes.
- Log into the NASA site on the Internet.
- Display pictures of different vehicles designed for different terrain (such as, a Lunar Rover, an ATV, a dune-buggy, a robotic spider).

Nicer...

Invite students to design and construct their own lunar landscape on which to test the vehicles.

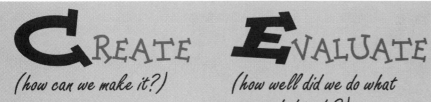

ACTIVITY 3E:

Shuttle Cockpit

For Your Interest

The Space Shuttle was developed in the 1970s to be a reusable piloted space vehicle. It's designed to be several vehicles in one: a rocket (for launching); a spacecraft (for orbiting the Earth); a truck (for carrying cargo); and an airplane (for landing back on Earth). The first orbital flights began in 1981. The shuttle continues today to be a useful vehicle for launching and repairing communications satellites.

Sparking Interest

- Show pictures of the shuttle in books and magazines.
- Load a suitable computer program that shows the launch and flight of the shuttle.
- Load and use a flight simulator program on the computer.
- Tell or invent a story about the shuttle.

Need

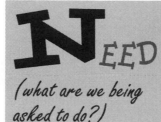

(what are we being asked to do?)

To make a space shuttle cockpit so that:

We can pretend to be astronauts on a mission.

OR We can show how an astronaut pilots a spacecraft.

Ideas

(what ideas do we have for doing it?)

- **What can we see inside the cockpit of the space shuttle?**

  For example:
  - chairs?
  - flashing lights?
  - dials and gauges?
  - something for steering?
  - windows?
  - something for talking to other people inside and outside the shuttle?
  - ?

- **What can we do or use to make the cockpit?**

  For example:
  - large cardboard box?
  - rearrange classroom furniture?
  - build it with paper logs?
  - ?

- **What can we do to make controls that light up or make sound?**

  For example:
  - use parts of old toys?
  - make them yourself?
  - research or review circuits and switches?
  - ?

- **What can we use for a steering control?**

  For example:
  - make or recycle a steering wheel?
  - make or recycle a joy stick?
  - ?

Create
(how can we make it?)

- **What materials would we want or need to build the cockpit?**

  For example:
  - cardboard from some appliance or furniture packing case?
  - cardboard tubes?
  - chairs?
  - ?

- **What tools and equipment do we need or want?**

  For example:
  - equipment from the bells and buzzers (electrical circuits) kit?
  - scissors?
  - paint?
  - recycled objects?
  - ?

Evaluate
(how well did we do what we needed to do?)

- **Does our cockpit have enough room for the astronauts to sit inside?**
- **Are the controls within reach of the astronauts?**
- **Can we explain how the controls in our cockpit work?**
- **Can we make the cockpit better? How?**

Nicer

Have students make astronaut costumes including helmets, gloves, and boots—for role playing in the cockpit.

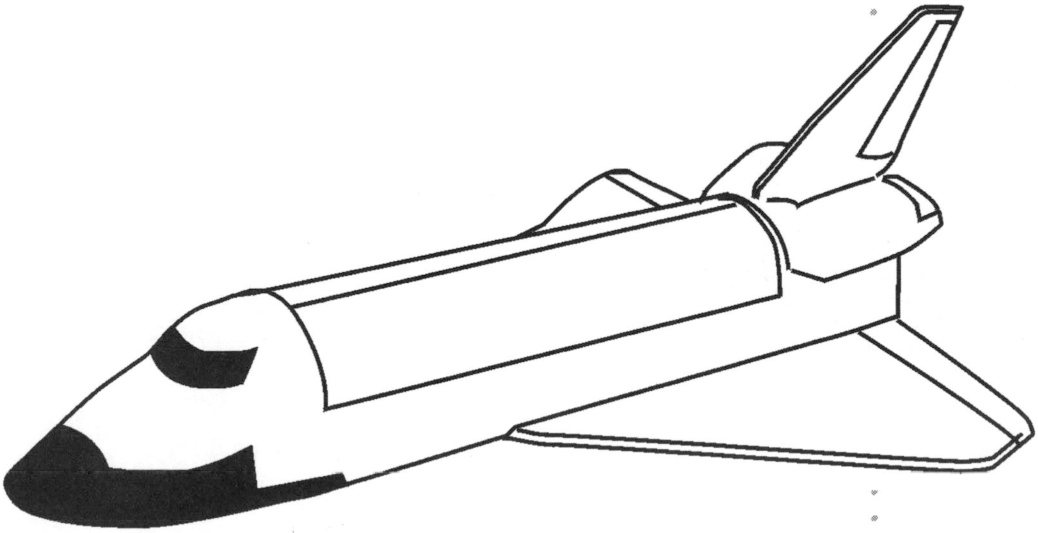

ACTIVITY 3F:

Star Games

For Your Interest

Games, whether for fun, for competition, or for education, provide wonderful opportunities for learning, developing, honing, and enhancing a wide variety of skills. It all depends on the type of game, of course, but consider even these few brief examples. Many board games sharpen problem-solving, as well as psychomotor skills. Any game played in teams is fertile ground for exercising social skills such as cooperation and disagreeing in an agreeable way. Clue-, riddle-, or recall-oriented games call upon a host of cognitive skills, as well as communication skills. And target-based games are great for eye-hand coordination.

NEED

(what are we being asked to do?)

To make a game about space so that:

We can review what we've learned about space.

OR We can help other people learn about space.

IDEAS

(what ideas do we have for doing it?)

- **What kind of games could we make?**

  For example:
  - board games?
  - card games?
  - computer games?
  - puzzles?
  - ?

- **What is the object of the game?**

  For example:
  - get to the moon?
  - get to the space station?
  - return safely to Earth from space?
  - gather more planets?
  - ?

- **What danger could be part of the game?**

  For example:
  - running out of fuel?
  - running out of air, water, food?
  - communications malfunction?
  - alien attack?
  - asteroid crash?
  - ?

- **How can we keep score?**

  For example:
  - points or counters?
  - moving spaces on a board?
  - collecting planets or stars?
  - ?

Create
(how can we make it?)

- **What materials do we need for the game and its container?**

  For example:
  - paper?
  - cardboard?
  - old game pieces?
  - old playing cards?
  - ?

- **What tools and equipment do we need or want?**

  For example:
  - do we need chips or markers for the players?
  - do we need dice?
  - do we need to build anything?
  - ?

Evaluate
(how well did we do what we needed to do?)

- **Do we enjoy playing the game?**
- **Are the rules clear and easy to follow?**
- **How easy is the game to put away and store?**
- **Could we make it better? How?**

Sparking Interest:

- Display a variety of games and discuss why people like to play them.
- Ask students to bring or describe their favourite game and say why they like it.
- Discuss the "learning" games in the classroom that the students like to play.

OTHER "IDEAS" OR "QUESTIONS" WE COULD THINK ABOUT

- How do we store the game when it isn't being used?
- What are the rules?
- How many players can play at one time?

Nicer

Challenge students to design a game that is made entirely out of recycled materials. Students might also enjoy creating a TV commercial and/or a magazine ad for their game.

UNIT 4

Pioneering

Activities:

4A: TOYS WERE US

4B: FOOD FOR THOUGHT

4C: TOOL TIME

4D: WEAVE YOUR OWN PLACEMAT

4E: SWAP SHOP

4F: BANK ON IT

4G: CROPPING US

ACTIVITY 4A:

Toys Were Us

For Your Interest

From the moment they're born, most children today grow up surrounded by toys of all kinds. But a century ago and more, toys purchased from a store were considered a luxury, far out of the economic reach of all but the very rich. Instead, children played with homemade toys, including those they made for themselves or their siblings. Many of the toys they played with—such as tops, dolls, stuffed animals, skipping ropes, hoops, and wagons—would be recognizable to children today.

Sparking Interest

- Show pictures or a video that illustrates the toys used by pioneer children.
- Read or tell a story about pioneer children at play.
- Display some hand made toys.
- Visit a pioneer museum and view the toys that children used in the past.

Need

(what are we being asked to do?)

To make toys that pioneer children might make so that:

We can imagine we're living in pioneer days.

OR We can play the way pioneer children played.

OR We can make our own pioneer toy museum in the classroom.

Ideas

(what ideas do we have for doing it?)

- **What types of toys do we think pioneer children had?**

  For example:
  - dolls?
  - stuffed animals?
  - tops?
  - skipping ropes?
  - wagons?
  - ?

- **What would these toys be made out of?**
  - wood?
  - rope?
  - fabric?
  - paper?
  - ?

- **What tools would pioneers have to make their toys?**
  - saws?
  - hammer and nails?
  - scissors?
  - needle and thread?
  - glue?
  - ?

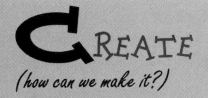

Create
(how can we make it?)

- **What materials can we use to make our pioneer toy?**

  For example:
  - – cardboard boxes?
  - – wooden crates?
  - – scraps of cloth?
  - – scrap wood
  - – string or wool?
  - – buttons?
  - – ?

- **What tools and equipment do we need or want?**

  For example:
  - – hammer and nails?
  - – glue?
  - – saw?
  - – scissors?
  - – paint?
  - – needle and thread?
  - – ?

Evaluate
(how well did we do what we needed to do?)

- **How does our toy work?**
- **How well can other children play with it?**
- **Can we make our toy better? How?**

OTHER "IDEAS" OR "QUESTIONS" WE COULD THINK ABOUT

- How would they decorate their toys to make them look interesting?
- How would they fasten their toys together?

Nicer

Invite students to make a display or a mural to compare toys of yesterday and today.

ACTIVITY 4B:

Food for Thought

For Your Interest

Some of our earliest technologies involve food—growing it (agriculture), cutting it, cooking it, and storing it. But in today's world of restaurants, grocery stores, and supermarkets, most students (certainly the urban ones) may find it hard to imagine the necessity of having to make such common staples as butter, jam, bread, and treats. Only 100 years ago fresh milk required a cow or goat (or a neighbour with one). Fresh fruit and vegetables required a garden to grow them. And unlike today, when seasonal produce such as lettuce or strawberries can be imported year-round, most fruit and vegetables were only available at certain times of the year.

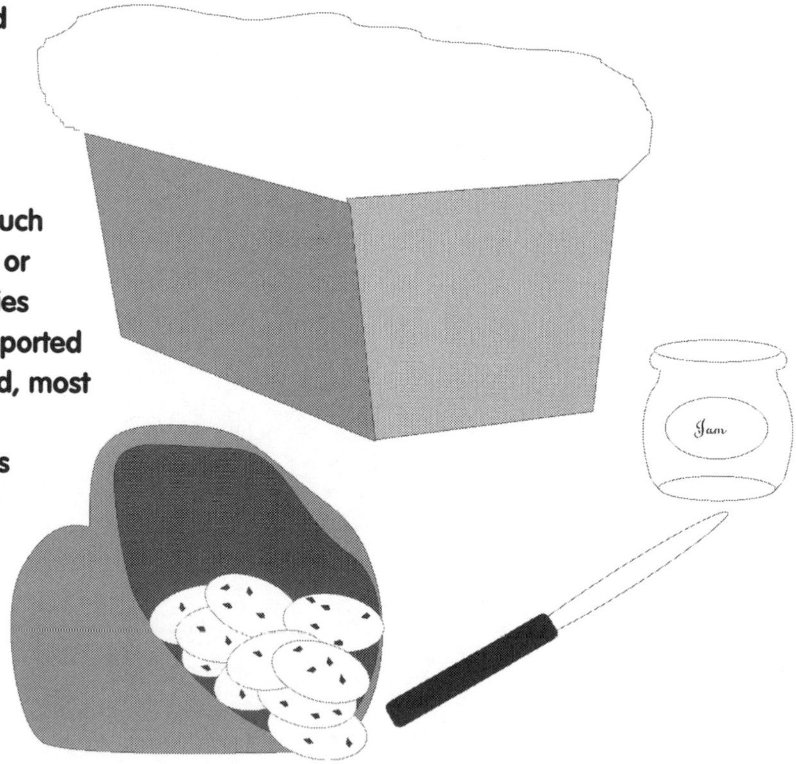

NEED

(what are we being asked to do?)

To make pioneer food so that:

We can taste the foods that pioneers ate.

OR We can have a pioneer feast.

IDEAS

(what ideas do we have for doing it?)

- **How is pioneer food different from what we eat today?**

  For example:
  - Did pioneer children have the same variety of foods we do?
  - Did they have the same foods available all year long?
  - Did they have restaurants to eat in?
  - Did they have refrigerators to keep foods fresh?
  - ?

- **Where can we find information about pioneer foods and recipes?**

  For example:
  - library books?
  - CD-ROM?
  - the Internet?
  - ask grandparents about their parents and grandparents?
  - ?

- **What kind of pioneer food do we want to make?**

  For example:
  - bread?
  - cookies?
  - jam?
  - ?

- **What ingredients will we need?**
  - This depends, of course, on what the class decides to make. See Appendix C for some recipe ideas.

CREATE
(how can we make it?)

- What recipe are we using?
- What ingredients do we need?
- What measuring equipment do we need?

  For example:
  - measuring cups?
  - measuring spoons?
  - thermometers?
  - scales?
  - ?
- What tools and equipment will we need?

  For example:
  - spoons?
  - spatulas?
  - forks?
  - knives?
  - beater?
  - mixing bowls?
  - ?

EVALUATE
(how well did we do what we needed to do?)

- How did we like the food we made?
- How did others like it?
- Could we make it better? How?

Nicer

Invite students to plan (and prepare) a pioneer banquet using recipes from their own cultural background. Students could also design and produce a pioneer cookbook using recipes from their own cultural backgrounds.

Sparking Interest

- Show a video or picture book which illustrates pioneer cooking and foods.
- Read or tell a story of pioneer family life in which the kitchen and cooking play a part.
- Visit a pioneer village to see how cookies, bread or other food was prepared.
- Collect pictures of pioneer kitchens and cooking implements.

ACTIVITY 4C:

Tool Time

For Your Interest

Preparing food, washing cloths, cleaning, gardening (in the yard or on an apartment balcony)—very few of the activities we do in and around the home today can be done without tools of one kind or another. Many of the tools used today are very different from those used by pioneers, yet their functions remain quite similar. Consider, for example, the wash bucket and scrub board, akin to today's automatic washer; the broom and rug beater perform the same basic function as a vacuum cleaner; a horse and plough do for the pioneer what a rototiller does for us; and the fireplace or wood stove has now been largely replaced by an electric or gas range.

Sparking Interest

- Show a video or picture book that illustrates the tools used in and around the home in pioneer days.
- Read or tell a story about pioneer days that focuses on some of the chores that they performed.
- Collect pictures or examples of old tools used in and around the pioneer home.
- Visit a pioneer village or museum to view the tools and possibly see them in use.

NEED
(what are we being asked to do?)

Make a display of pioneer tools so that:

We can decorate our classroom for the pioneer unit.

OR We can show the types of tools used in pioneer days.

IDEAS
(what ideas do we have for doing it?)

- **Where can we look for information about tools pioneers used?**

  For example:
  - in library reference books?
  - on a CD-ROM?
  - at a local historical museum?
  - on a TV show?
  - ?

- **How can we show other people what these tools looked like?**

  For example:
  - draw pictures?
  - make models?
  - colour, cut, paste, and print clip art?
  - ?

- **How can we display the things we learn about tools for others to see?**

  For example:
  - in a scrap book?
  - on a poster?
  - on a mural?
  - in a mobile?
  - in a play or skit using the model tools?
  - ?

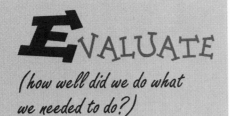

CREATE
(how can we make it?)

- **What materials and equipment do we need if we make a scrapbook:**

  For example:
  - scissors?
  - paper?
  - glue or tape?
  - ?
- **if we make a mural?**

  For example:
  - mural paper?
  - paint?
  - coloured paper?
  - ?
- **if we make a mobile?**

  For example:
  - paper?
  - string?
  - scissors?
  - old plastic containers?
  - ?
- **if we make models?**

  For example:
  - old broom handles?
  - papier maché?
  - wood?
  - saws?
  - ?

EVALUATE
(how well did we do what we needed to do?)

- **Does the display give people a good idea of the kinds of tools pioneers used?**
- **Are the tools easy to recognize or identify?**
- **Could the display be improved? How?**

Nicer

Invite students to choose a pioneer tool that has evolved to a new modern equivalent and predict changes that may occur to the tool or appliance in the future.

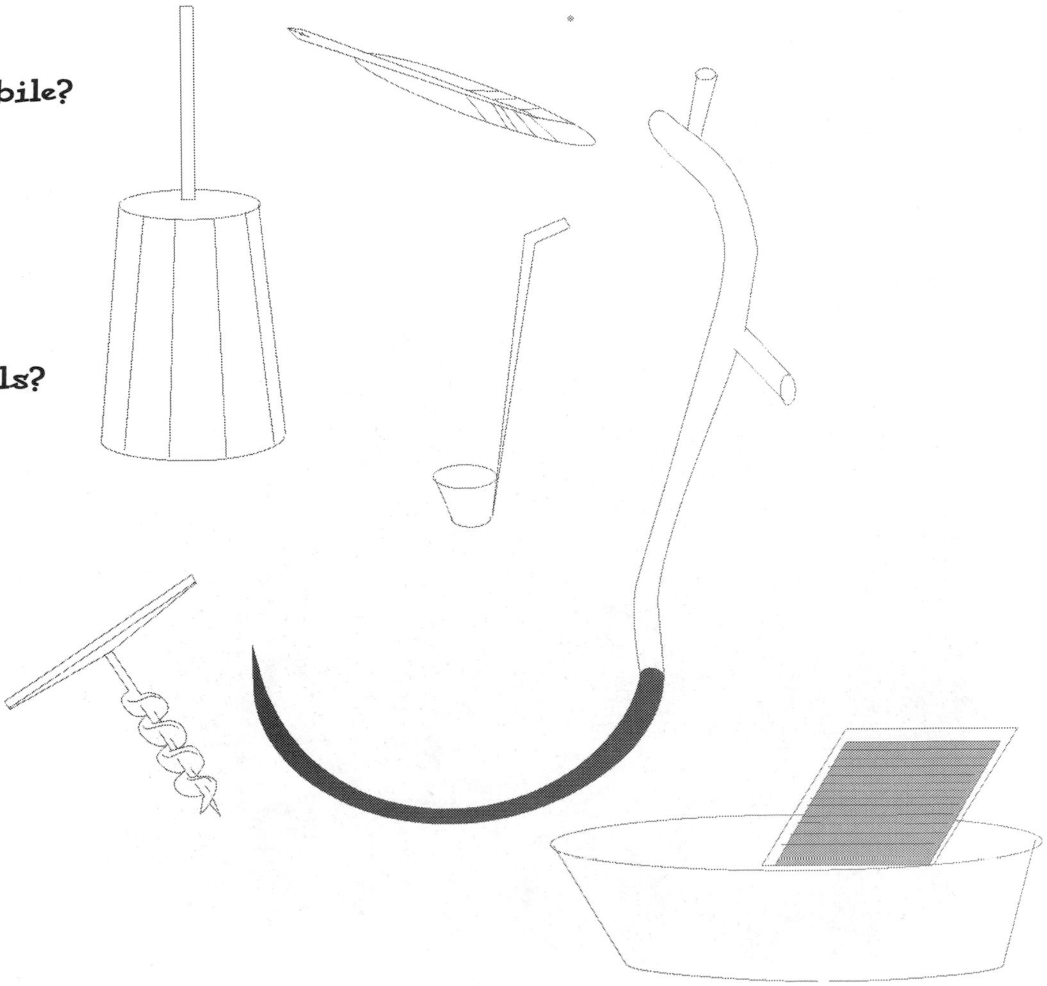

ACTIVITY 4D:

Weave Your Own Placemat

For Your Interest

Weaving is an ancient technology common to most cultures around the world. However, it is not a "self-evident" technology in the sense that young children will be able to infer or develop it on their own. So:

We recommend having students do some preliminary research on weaving (and possibly simple loom designs) in order make their pioneer placemats. One particularly good resource, if your school or local library has it, is the Recyclopedia: Games, Science Equipment, and Crafts from Recycled Materials, by Robin Simons, Houghton Mifflin, 1976, pages 82–93.

Sparking Interest

- Look at samples of fabric under a magnifying lens.
- Visit a pioneer
- Display pictures of weaving found in nature (such as the nests of birds, such as orioles or weaver birds, or stickle back fish) to see that other kinds of animals besides humans weave.

NEED

(what are we being asked to do?)

To make a pioneer placemat so that:

We can eat our lunch on it.
OR We can take it home to decorate our table.

IDEAS

(what ideas do we have for doing it?)

- **Where can we gather information on weaving?**

For example:
- library reference books?
- CD-ROM's?
- the Internet?
- a local museum or pioneer village?
- senior citizens such as relatives or people in a retirement home?
- ?

- **How can we decide what kind of weaving to try?**

For example:
- practise following instructions from a book or computer?
- get someone who knows how to show you?
- form groups to share information and experiment with different ways to weave?
- ?

- **What shape would we like our placemat to be?**

For example:
- square?
- rectangular?
- round?
- ?

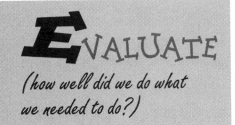

CREATE
(how can we make it?)

- **What materials can we use?**

  For example:
  - construction paper?
  - yarn?
  - strips of old fabric?
  - leaves?
  - pieces of straw?
  - feathers?
  - soft twigs?
  - ?

- **How can we make interesting designs?**

  For example:
  - decide on an interesting shape for the placemat?
  - use weaving strips that have different widths?
  - use weaving strips that have different shapes?
  - use a variety of materials for weaving strips?
  - use weaving strips that have different colours?
  - ?

EVALUATE
(how well did we do what we needed to do?)

- **Did our placemat design work out the way we wanted it to?**
- **Who else in the class had interesting or successful designs?**
- **Could we make our placemat better? How?**

Nicer

Invite students to design and build their own looms for weaving other kinds of textiles, or to find out how to weave (braid) friendship bracelets or necklaces.

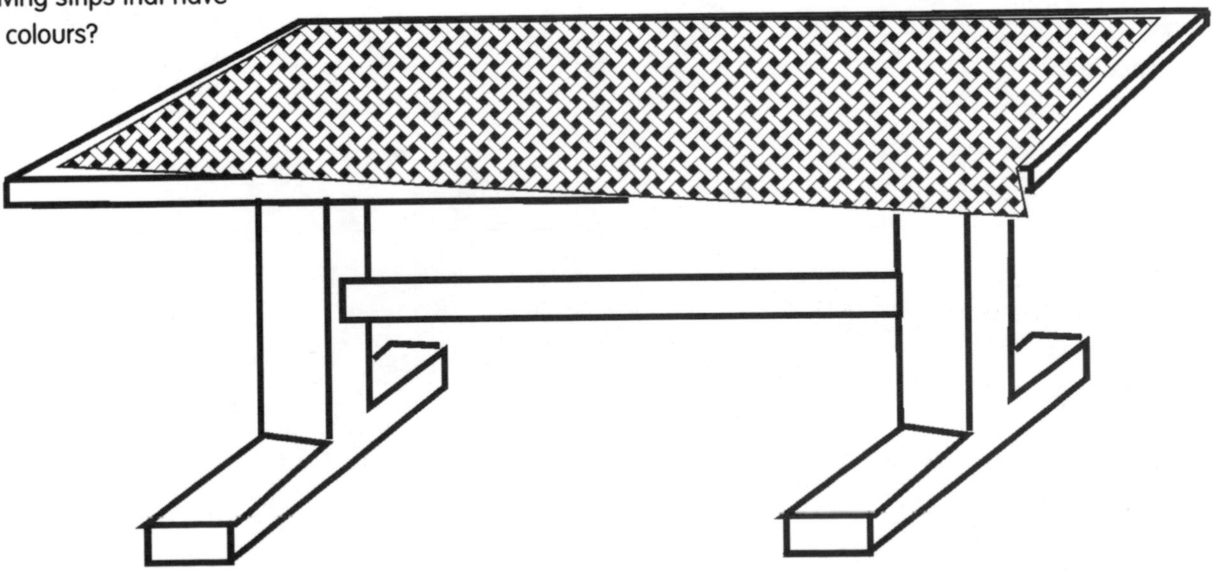

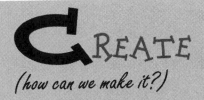

ACTIVITY 4E:

Swap Shop

For Your Interest

The general store or trading post was the centre of activity for many pioneer villages and towns. This was the place where native peoples, trappers, and farmers could exchange their goods for manufactured products which were brought into the village from far away. The general store/trading post was a place where people could get local news as well as pick up and send their mail. It stocked medical supplies, candy, dry goods, hardware, sewing supplies, clothing, and footwear. Often the trading post or general store was set up at a crossroads or on a main transportation route. The owner of a general store frequently played the role of banker in many small communities by giving credit to local people so that the community could survive in hard times.

NEED

(what are we being asked to do?)

To set up a general store so that:

We can show what early traders and merchants would sell or trade in the olden days.

OR We can show how these early merchants could store and display their products.

OR We can play or perform a skit about pioneers trading.

IDEAS

(what ideas do we have for doing it?)

- **How can we show what the store looked like?**

  For example:
  - make a model to show the inside of the store?
  - draw pictures of the store?
  - make a diorama of the store?
  - decorate our classroom like a store?
  - ?

- **What products will we sell?**

  For example:
  - food stuff?
  - hardware?
  - clothing?
  - sewing supplies?
  - medicine?

- **What products will we accept for trade?**

  For example:
  - furs?
  - farm produce?
  - gold?
  - ?

CREATE
(how can we make it?)

- **What can we use to make the storage containers?**

  For example:
  - cardboard or cardboard boxes
  - construction paper?
  - wood?
  - ?

EVALUATE
(how well did we do what we needed to do?)

- **Does the display give people a good idea of what a trading post or general store was like?**
- **Could we make it better? How?**

OTHER "CREATE" IDEAS

- What can we use to make the goods which we will be selling?
- Will we need signs?
- What will we use to keep our money in?

OTHER "IDEAS" OR "QUESTIONS" WE COULD THINK ABOUT

- How will we display items so customers will want to buy them?
- What will we call the store/trading post?
- How will we keep the store warm in winter?
- Will there be room for people to sit and talk? What will they sit on?

Nicer

Invite the students to develop a play which would show how a merchant might bargain during a trade with a trapper or a farmer.

Sparking Interest

- Visit a pioneer village or museum to view the general store/trading post and note the products and how they were stored.
- Collect and display pictures of a modern supermarket, drug store, hardware store, etc. to show how products are stored and presented.
- Show a video which depicts life in and around the general store/trading post.

ACTIVITY 4F:

Bank on It

For Your Interest

Coins have existed for at least 3000 years. Before coins, precious metals, jewels, and animals would have been used for trade. (And they still are: in Papua, New Guinea, for example, both the domesticated pig and the flightless bird, the Cassowary, are considered to be as valuable in many areas as money.) Storing and protecting their money has been a concern of people from the very beginning. There are records on clay tablets, dating back 4000 years, of institutions where people could store their money for a price.

Before banking institutions, precious metals, coins, and jewels were kept hidden in pouches, boxes, and jars. Today, coins are still kept in a variety of containers, not so much to hide them from robbers but to store them or save them. Many of these storage containers or banks come in various decorative shapes and sizes. The "classic" storage bank is the piggy bank.

NEED

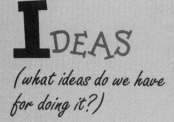

(what are we being asked to do?)

To make a pioneer "piggy bank" so that:

We can deposit and save money.

OR We can have a gift to give a friend.

IDEAS

(what ideas do we have for doing it?)

- **What other shapes could the bank be besides a pig?**

For example:
- cow?
- horse?
- sheep?
- dog?
- cat?
- barn?
- ?

OTHER "IDEAS" OR "QUESTIONS" WE COULD THINK ABOUT

- How big does the slot or hole need to be to get the money in but to keep it from falling out?
- Where will the money slot or hole go in the bank?
- How can we get the money out without breaking or ruining the bank?
- Will our bank have any moving parts?
- What parts will move?
- How will they move?

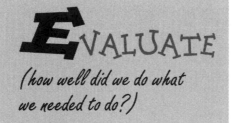

CREATE
(how can we make it?)

- **What materials can we use?**

  For example:
  - fabric?
  - papier maché?
  - construction paper?
  - a shoe box?
  - an old boot?
  - ?
- **How will we decorate it?**

  For example:
  - paint?
  - buttons?
  - ribbons?
  - feathers?
  - ?
- **What tools and equipment do we need to make it?**

  For example:
  - scissors?
  - glue?
  - paste?
  - needle and thread?
  - ?

EVALUATE
(how well did we do what we needed to do?)

- **Can we put money in easily?**
- **Can we get it out easily?**
- **Could we make our bank better? How?**

Nicer

Invite the students to create a model of a a teller's cage in a pioneer bank and role-play depositing money.

Sparking Interest

- Collect and display different types of coin banks.
- Read or tell a story about a piggy bank.

ACTIVITY 4G:

Cropping Up

For Your Interest

Starting roughly 10,000 years ago, people began deliberately to plant and grow specific plants to use for food. This practice marked the start of one of humanity's major technological innovations: farming (agriculture).

Farming nicely illustrates the "dual" nature of technology as both product and process. Tools and equipment such as shovels, hoes, threshers, and combines are all examples of technological products (devices), while techniques such as irrigation, crop-rotation, applying fertilizers, and mulching are all examples of technological processes. Both have the same practical purpose —to cultivate and harvest plants for us (and our domesticated animals) to eat.

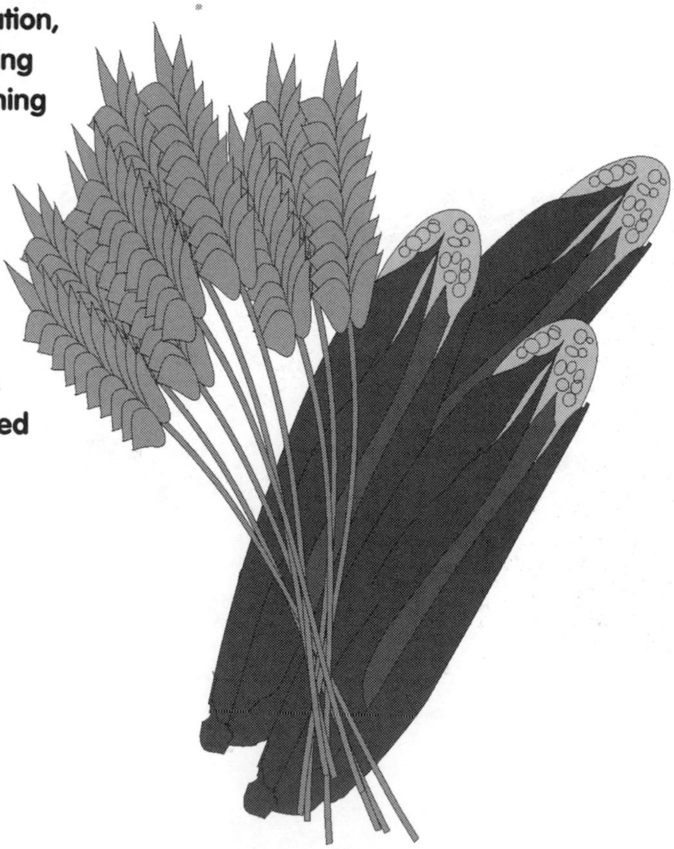

NEED

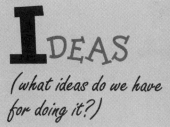

(what are we being asked to do?)

To set up a mini farm field so that:

We can grow our own crops.
OR We can experiment with growing plants.

IDEAS

(what ideas do we have for doing it?)

- **Will we grow our crops from seeds?**
- **Will we grow our crops using baby plants?**
- **What do crops need to grow?**
  For example:
  - water?
  - sunlight?
  - soil?
  - air?
  - nutrients?
  - ?
- **How can we find out what to do to grow our crops?**
  For example:
  - read the seed package?
  - gather information from the library (or CD–ROM or a commercial plant nursery?)
  - read or talk to someone about soil?
  - ?
- **How can everyone take part in this activity?**
  For example:
  - share responsibilities?
  - assign different roles?
  - each grows their own plants?
  - ?

CREATE
(how can we make it?)

- **What kind of crops will we grow?**

  For example:
  - radishes?
  - beans or bean sprouts?
  - mint (or oregano, parsley, or other easy-to-grow herbs)?
  - onions?
  - ?

- **What do we need to grow our crops?**

  For example:
  - a container (such as a planting tray)?
  - soil?
  - a sunny place? (or a grow-light?)
  - container for watering?
  - popsicle sticks to label the crops?
  - ?

EVALUATE
(how well did we do what we needed to do?)

- **How well did our crops grow?**
- **If there were problems, what did we do to solve them?**
- **If we were going to start again, what would we do differently? Why?**

Sparking Interest

- Read a story (such as Peter Rabbit) about a farmer and garden or field.
- Collect and display vegetable seed packages or pictures from a seed catalogue.
- Visit a market garden or a local farm fair to view the prize produce.

Nicer

Invite the students to use their produce in a cooking project such as Friendship Soup (see Family & Friends theme).

UNIT 5

Time

Activities:

5A: HICKORY DICKORY DOCK

5B: THE BEAT GOES ON

5C: BACKTRACKING

5D: RACE AGAINST TIME

5E: GET THERE ON TIME

5F: SLOWER THAN MOLASSES

5G: A MEMORY-TREASURE TIMELINE

▶ Time

ACTIVITY 5A:

Hickory Dickory Clock

For Your Interest

We need to be able to tell time for many practical reasons. We have to get to school and to work on time. Some people need to take medicine at a certain time. We like to watch our favourite TV shows so we need to know when they are on. If we need to take a train and plane we must be at the station or airport on time.

Clocks come in two basic formats: analog and digital. Analog clocks usually have a dial on which hands move. Digital clocks tell the time with numbers that change every second, minute, and hour. Despite the prevalence of digital clocks today (on computers, VCRs, and TVs, for example), the old, trusty "clock-with-hands" continues to hold its own for time-telling. So learning how to read an analog clock is—pardon the pun—time well spent!

NEED (what are we being asked to do?)

To make a model of a clock so that:

- We can practice telling the time.

IDEAS (what ideas do we have for doing it?)

- **What shape will our clock be?**

  For example:
  - round?
  - square?
  - diamond-shaped?
  - ?

- **How many hands do we need?**
  - a minute hand?
  - an hour hand?
  - a second hand?

- **How can we put the numbers in the right place?**

  For example:
  - trace over a real clock?
  - trace over a picture of a clock?
  - ?

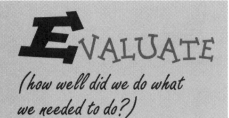

CREATE
(how can we make it?)

- **What materials could we use?**

  For example:
  - for the clock face?
  - for the hands?
  - for the numbers?
- **What tools or equipment do we need?**

  For example:
  - scissors?
  - paper clips?
  - plywood?
  - paint?
  - glue?
  - ?

EVALUATE
(how well did we do what we needed to do?)

- **Does the model look like a real clock?**
- **Do the hands move?**
- **Are the numbers readable?**
- **Could we make our clock better? How?**

OTHER "IDEAS" OR "QUESTIONS" WE COULD THINK ABOUT

- How will we attach the hands so they can move?
- Will we make it stand up or hang from the wall?

Nicer

Challenge students to develop a clock that actually tracks time. It could be something like a sundial which can be used to tell various times during the day or something that can measure smaller discrete time periods like an egg timer or hour glass.

Sparking Interest

- Discuss things that have clocks built into them such as VCRs and coffee makers.
- Discuss why people want or need to measure ("tell") time.

ACTIVITY 5B:

The Beat Goes On

For Your Interest

Percussion instruments (those that make sound by striking one thing against another—such as bells, rattles, drums, cymbals, xylophones, pianos)—are used to maintain music's rhythmic beat. The beat lets musicians keep in time with each other, and its repetitive pattern is, in part, what makes music pleasing to the ear. Our sensitivity to rhythmic beating begins early, in the womb, where we all were lulled by our mothers' beating hearts. (This may explain why the drum, in one form or another, is common virtually to all cultures, past and present, around the world.) To appreciate the power of the beat in action, just watch the swaying bodies and moving feet, legs, hands, and fingers of people "in tune" with time counted out in musical beats.

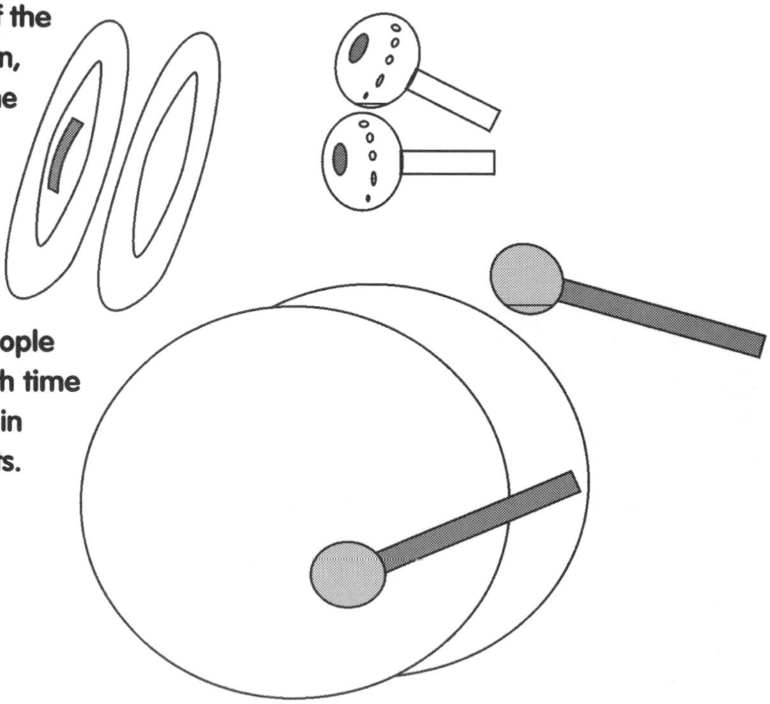

Need

(what are we being asked to do?)

To make a rhythm instrument so that:

We can play along with the songs we sing.

OR We can compose and play music.

OR We can experiment with different rhythm beats.

Ideas

(what ideas do we have for doing it?)

- **How do people keep time with the beat of music?**

  For example:
  - clap hands?
  - snap fingers?
  - stomp feet?
  - ?

- **What are some examples of instruments that help keep time with music?**

  For example:
  - drums?
  - tambourines?
  - maracas?
  - ?

- **What kinds of sounds do these instruments make?**

  For example:
  - rattling sounds?
  - booming sounds?
  - jingling sounds?
  - ?

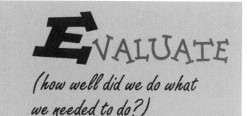

CREATE
(how can we make it?)

- **What materials do we need?**

  For example:
  To make a drum:
  – what's the body?
  – what's the skin?
  – what will we hit it with?
  To make a rattle:
  – what makes the noise?
  – what will hold the noise-makers?
- **What tools and equipment do we need?**

  For example:
  – wood?
  – saw?
  – papier maché?
  – old plastic containers?
  – ?

EVALUATE
(how well did we do what we needed to do?)

- **Is our instrument loud enough? (Too loud?)**
- **Can we use it to keep time for songs we like?**
- **How easy is it to play?**
- **Could we make it better? How?**

OTHER "IDEAS" OR "QUESTIONS" WE COULD THINK ABOUT

- What's similar about the way beat-keeping instruments work?
- How could we design our own beat-keeping instrument?
- Will we want or need to decorate our instrument?

Nicer

Challenge the students to develop a selection of rhythm pieces with their instruments that they could present to other classes.

Sparking Interest

- Show videotapes of commercials that feature percussion sounds (such as Rubbermaid, Suzuki Side Kick, Pringles Potato Chips)
- Play some music that emphasizes percussion (such as Tchaikovsky's 1812 Overture, Strauss' Thus Spake Zarathustra, or Queen's We Will Rock You.
- Collect pictures of rhythm instruments.
- Load a suitable software program (such as an encyclopedia) that shows different musical instruments and plays their musical sounds.

ACTIVITY 5C:

Back-tracking

For Your Interest

Many of our ideas about dinosaurs have changed since the first bones were discovered in the 1820s. Most scientists today believe that dinosaurs were warm-blooded, and that they are more closely related to birds than to reptiles. Fossils of eggs, regurgitated food, and nests suggest certain species may have cared for their young like birds (and a very few reptiles) do. Fossils of skin provide clues about texture. We even imagine colours for these long-dead animals, based on observing animals today in their habitats. But the key word here is "imagine." The major difference between how scientists and children might picture a dinosaur is in their depth of knowledge and thinking skills. This reliance on imagination may account for the fascination people of all ages continue to have with dinosaurs.

NEED

(what are we being asked to do?)

To make a model of a dinosaur so that:

We can imagine what they might have looked like.

OR We can show how they might have lived.

OR We can set up our own "Dinosaur Park."

IDEAS

(what ideas do we have for doing it?)

- **How big should the model be?**

For example:
– big enough to fit on our desks?
– as high as the room?
– as big as us?
– ?

- **What should it look like?**

For example:
– will it have scales?
– will it have teeth?
– will it have claws?
– will it have a long neck or a short neck?
– ?

OTHER "IDEAS" OR "QUESTIONS" WE COULD THINK ABOUT

- What colour or colours should it be?
- Will it stand on its back legs or on all four legs?
- Will any of its parts (tail, legs, mouth) be able to move?

Sparking Interest

- Show pictures of dinosaurs, or a clip from a movie or TV show that depicts dinosaurs.
- Load a suitable computer program that shows current information about dinosaurs, or drop in on a museum web site.
- Tell or invent a story about a dinosaur.
- Display a model or toy dinosaur.

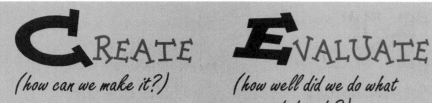

Create
(how can we make it?)

- **What materials would be good for building the dinosaur?**

  For example:
  - cardboard boxes?
  - cardboard tubes?
  - construction paper?
  - fabric?
  - papier maché?
  - ?

- **What tools or equipment do we need or want?**

  For example:
  - scissors?
  - glue?
  - tape?
  - paint?
  - ?

- **How can we make any part of it moveable?**

  For example:
  - use cloth at the joint?
  - make a hinge with tape?
  - attach the moving part with string?
  - ?

Evaluate
(how well did we do what we needed to do?)

- **Does our dinosaur look real?**
- **Do any of the other models made in our class look different? How are they different?**
- **Could we make our dinosaur better? How?**

Nicer

Invite students to measure the hallways and mark out and label actual lengths of real dinosaurs. If the building is high enough, ask them to determine where the Tyrannosaur's or the Diplodocus head would be on the side of the school.

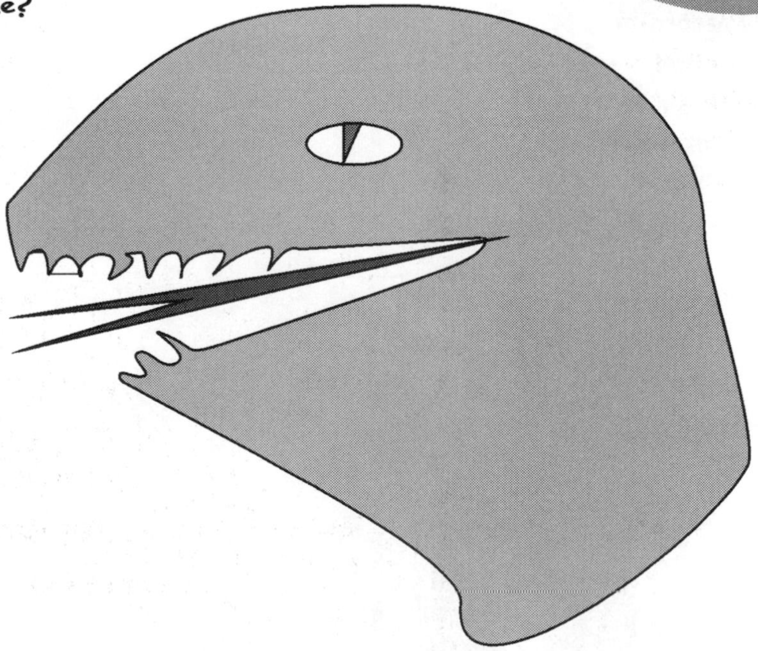

ACTIVITY 5D:

Race against Time

For Your Interest

In 1862 the first successful car powered by an internal combustion engine was created by Etienne Lenoire in France. (Combustion means burning. Basically the force created by a fuel being burned explosively in a confined space, over and over again, pushes the car forward.) The first practical automobile was created by Carl Benz in Germany in 1885. One year earlier, the world's first car race took place in France. The average speed of the vehicles was 16 km/h (10 mph). In 1905 Louis Chevrolet set a speed record of 109 km/h (68 mph). The first speedway, an oval track for car racing, was built in England in 1906. The Indianapolis Speedway, where the Indy 500 has been run annually since, was built in 1911. In the first Indy race the cars averaged less than 120 km/h (75 mph). Today they run at more than twice that speed with an average about 240 km/h (150 mph).

NEED

(what are we being asked to do?)

To build a model car so that:

We can test its speed.
OR We can learn about car designs.
OR We can have a toy to play with.

IDEAS

(what ideas do we have for doing it?)

- **How will we test the cars?**

For example:
– roll them down a ramp?
– push them on the floor?
– use an elastic to push them along the floor?
– ?

- **How big should it be?**

For example:
– big enough to fit in a shoe box or a pencil box?
– as long as a ruler?
– big enough to fit on the ramp?
– ?

- **What should it look like?**

For example:
– long and thin or short and fat?
– big wheels or small?
– what colour?
– ?

CREATE
(how can we make it?)

- **What materials would be good to make the car?**

  For example:
  - construction kits?
  - cardboard boxes?
  - wood blocks?
  - ?
- **What would be good for the wheels?**

  For example:
  - bottle tops/jar lids?
  - wheels from old toys?
  - commercial wooden wheels?
  - carrot slices?
  - ?
- **How can we attach the wheels to the vehicle so they can turn?**

  For example:
  - barbecue skewers for axles?
  - nails for axles?
  - straws for bearings?
  - ?
- **How can we decorate the car?**

  For example:
  - paint?
  - stickers?
  - marker or crayon?
  - stripes, flames, or numbers?
  - ?

EVALUATE
(how well did we do what we needed to do?)

- **How far or fast did our car go?**
- **Did our car go straight or did it turn?**
- **Did other cars made in the class roll farther or faster? Why?**
- **Could we make our car better? How?**

OTHER "IDEAS" OR "QUESTIONS" WE COULD THINK ABOUT

- Should it be heavy or light?
- Where should the driver sit?
- Are we designing to see how fast the car goes, or how far, or both?

Nicer

Invite your class to display their vehicles in a "car show." They may want to develop a display stand or make signs or trophies to enhance their display.

Sparking Interest

- Collect and display pictures of race cars.
- Display models of racing cars.
- Read or make up a story about a racing car.
- Show a film or video of a car race.

ACTIVITY 5E:

Get There on Time

For Your Interest

There are many kinds of schedules that people use to help organize their busy lives. Bus, train, and plane timetables are schedules. TV and radio program start times are printed in schedules. Baseball games are scheduled well in advance. Business people, doctors, and teachers have to plan their days, too. Their schedule is kept in a book sometimes referred to as a daytimer. From October through January, stationery and business supply stores have large selections of these time organizers or diaries. There has recently been increased growth in the electronic version of the daytimer. Computer programs and dedicated pocket organizers are available in all price ranges.

Sparking Interest

- Display pictures or advertisements of schedule organizers.
- Collect a variety of different diaries for your students to examine.
- Display bus and train schedules, TV and radio schedules, sports schedules, etc.

NEED

(what are we being asked to do?)

To make a personal planner that we can use to:

Plan your week.
OR Record important events that we have done.
OR Record any school work that we may need to do.

IDEAS

(what ideas do we have for doing it?)

- **How long will we need to keep the planner?**

  For example:
  - one week?
  - one month?
  - ?

- **What information will we need to keep track of?**

  For example:
  - homework or school assignments?
  - club meetings?
  - music lessons or sporting events?
  - favourite TV programs?
  - family visits or trips?
  - special classes like gym, art, or music?
  - ?

- **What other information needs to be in the planner?**

  For example:
  - our name?
  - our school?
  - our address or class?
  - our phone number?
  - phone numbers of our friends?
  - ?

CREATE
(how can we make it?)

- **How will we plan the look of our personal planner?**

  For example:
  - one page per day?
  - two pages for a week?
  - blank pages for writing information?
  - lines for writing on?
  - squares to fill in?
  - day divided into morning and afternoon?
  - day divided into hours?
  - ?
- **How will the pages be fastened?**

  For example:
  - staples?
  - duotang cover?
  - string?
  - cerlox binding?
  - ?

OTHER "CREATE" QUESTIONS WE COULD THINK ABOUT

- How many pages do we need?
- Do we want to design it on the computer?
- What will the cover look like?
- Do we need a pencil holder built in?

EVALUATE
(how well did we do what we needed to do?)

- **Did your planner hold all the necessary information well?**
- **Were we able to follow the schedule? What happened if we planned to do something but couldn't?**
- **Did we do some things that we didn't have a chance to write in? Why?**
- **Could we make our planner better? How?**

Nicer

Invite students to create a map-size planner for classroom activities and events.

Monday

7:00 am	Breakfast
8:00	Catch school bus
8:30	Meet friends and play at school
9:00	Work at school
10:00	Recess
10:15	Back to work
12:00	Lunch
12:20	Play in yard
1:00 pm	Back to work
2:15	Recess
2:30	Recess is over.
3:30	Get on bus
4:00	Home for a snack
4:15	Play with friends
5:30	Supper time
6:30	Bath Time
7:00	Watch TV
9:00	Bed Time

ACTIVITY 5F:

Slower Than Molasses

For Your Interest

It's often necessary to slow an object or an action down. Cars need to be slowed down and stopped when they approach a stop light. Airplanes need to slow down before they can land safely. When children slide down the playground slide they need to slow down at the bottom or they might hurt themselves.

The braking action for most physical motion involves increasing friction between the moving object and the surface on which, or medium through which, the object is moving. In cars, the brake shoes rub against the disks or the drums in the wheels. This causes the wheels to slow their rotation. For planes, the friction between the air and the plane is increased when the flaps are lowered. The children on slides use their hands and or feet to create friction on the sides of the slide to slow their descent.

NEED

(what are we being asked to do?)

To make a braking system for a vehicle so that:

We can make it roll as slowly as possible down a ramp.

OR We can investigate friction.

OR We can have slow races.

IDEAS

(what ideas do we have for doing it?)

- **Are we making a new vehicle or using one that has already been made?**
- **How will we test the braking system of our vehicles?**

  For example:
  - roll them down a ramp?
  - push them on the floor?
  - use an elastic to push them along the floor?
  - ?
- **How can we make the wheels turn slower?**

  For example:
  - make the hole for the axle smaller?
  - make the wheels treads sticky?
  - make them less round?
  - make them rub against the vehicle?
- **What other slowing-down ideas do we have?**

  For example:
  - add something that will rub against the ground?
  - change the shape of the vehicle?
  - make the vehicle lighter or heavier?
  - ?

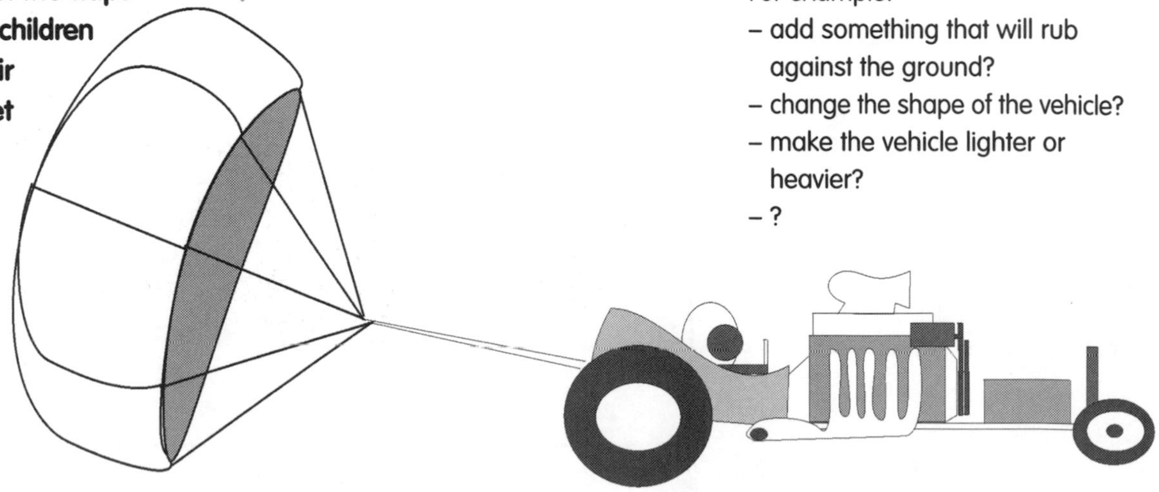

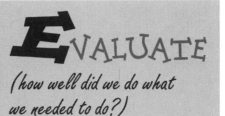

Create
(how can we make it?)

- **What can we do to make the wheels turn slower?**

  For example:
  - glue the holes to make them smaller?
  - add tape or paper to the wheel bearings to make them tight?
  - add flaps of paper to the wheels to rub against the body of the vehicle?
  - add studs or bumps to the wheel surfaces to make them rough?
  - ?

- **What can we add to the body that will make the vehicle move slower?**

  For example:
  - air flaps?
  - a parachute?
  - a brake to drag on the ground?
  - ?

- **What materials would be good to make the brake devices?**

  For example:
  - construction paper?
  - fabric?
  - string?
  - glue and/or tape?
  - ?

Evaluate
(how well did we do what we needed to do?)

- **Did our vehicle roll slowly? Did it move at all?**
- **Did any braking systems made in our class work differently than yours? How?**
- **Did any of the other braking systems work better than yours? How?**
- **Could we make our braking system better? How?**

Nicer

Invite your class to make parachutes that will allow a small object to fall slowly to the ground after it's been thrown in the air.

Sparking Interest

- Show a bicycle with hand brakes and demonstrate their operation.
- Bring in some in–line skates or figure skates to show the friction pad or picks are used for stopping.
- Show a video of skydiving or the return of a space capsule with a parachute.

ACTIVITY 5G:

A Memory-Treasure Timeline

For Your Interest

People like to know about their family history. They save pictures and family heirlooms as a reminder of their past. And they organize these "memory-treasures" in a variety of ways—for example, chronologically arranged photo albums, curio cabinet displays, family "trees" or pedigree charts, and simple linear timelines—so that present and future generations can trace all the names of the family members and see how they are related. Note: In doing this activity, it is, of course, very important to consider the make-up of your class. Being aware of and sensitive to issues such as adoption and foster care will influence how you conduct this activity in your classroom.

Sparking Interest

- Display collections of photographs of two or three generations of a family.
- Discuss any obvious changes in fashions and technology over time in the photos (black & white photos, cars appliances or furnishings in the backgrounds, types of clothing worn by people in the photos, etc.).

Need

(what are we being asked to do?)

To make a personal family history so that:

We can see how things have changed during our lives.

OR We can see how our family has grown or changed.

Ideas

(what ideas do we have for doing it?)

- **Where can we get information about our family?**

  For example:
  - interview our parents?
  - look in family photograph albums?
  - collect stories from grandparents or other relatives?
  - read old diaries or journals kept by our family?
  - look at old report cards and other documents that family members have saved?
  - ?

- **Where will the family history begin?**

  For example:
  - when we were born?
  - when our parents were married?
  - when our parents were born?
  - with our grandparents?
  - ?

- **How detailed will the family history be?**

  For example:
  - will it include our brothers and sisters?
  - will it include our cousins, aunts, and uncles?
  - ?

- **What important events should be included?**

  For example:
  - birthdays?
  - weddings?
  - beginning schools, graduations, etc.?
  - holidays, vacations, etc.?
  - ?

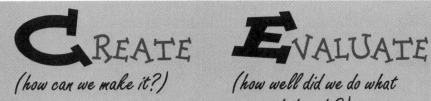

Create (how can we make it?)

- **What will our family history timeline look like?**

  For example:
  - will it be a poster?
  - a flowchart?
  - a bulletin board?
  - ?

- **What will we include?**

  For example:
  - photographs?
  - names?
  - dates?
  - medals, trophies, or other family treasures (that is, items that commemorate family members' accomplishments)?
  - ?

- **What tools and equipment do we need?**

  For example:
  - ruler?
  - marking pens?
  - tape or glue?
  - computer software?
  - scanner and printer?
  - ?

Evaluate (how well did we do what we needed to do?)

- **Does the family history present information clearly?**
- **Are other family histories in the class displayed differently from yours? How?**
- **Could we improve it? How?**

Nicer

Invite the students to collaborate on a technology timeline display. This may be based on dolls, toys, or games that have been collected at home, or on pictures and photographs that they find in books and albums.

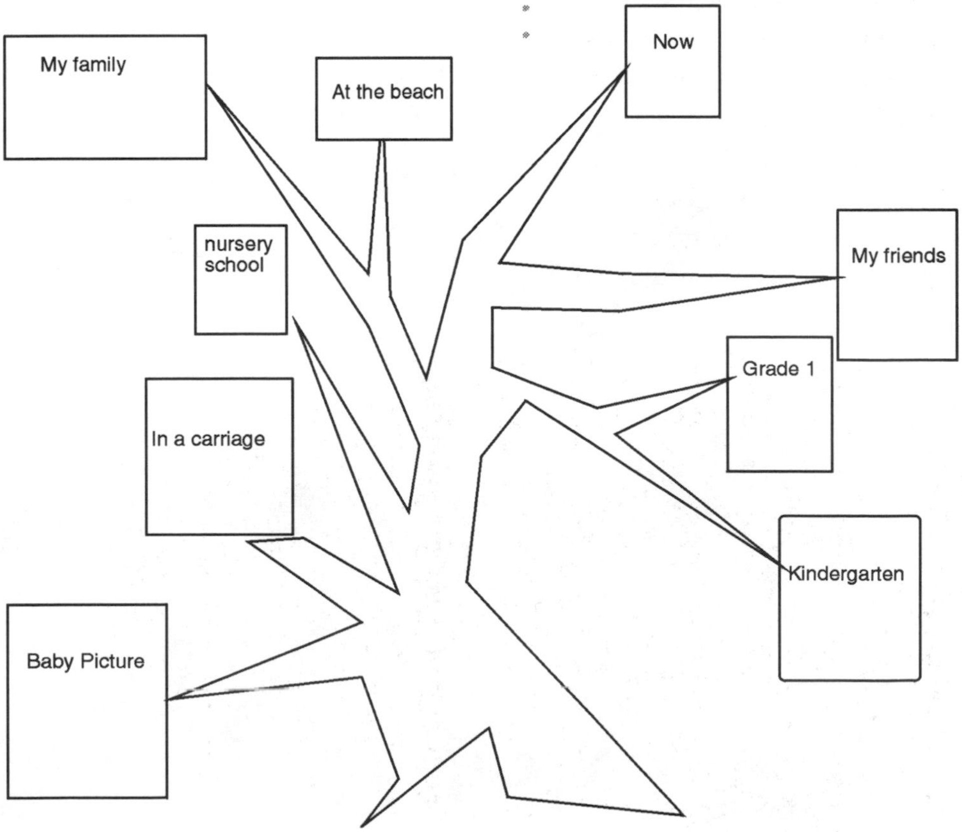

UNIT 6

Family & Friends

Activities:

6 A: SUN HAT

6 B: GOODIES FROM GRANDMA

6 C: FRIENDSHIP SOUP

6 D: GREETINGS FROM THE HEART

6 E: NOTHING TO DO?

6 F: TRY PUPPETRY

▶ Family & Friends

ACTIVITY 6A:

Sun Hat

Many technologies are solutions to practical problems related to the need to protect ourselves from the vagaries of climate and weather. For example, we have invented several different technologies for protecting our heads from the bright heat of sunlight. Any free-standing structure—for example, a bus shelter, a covered porch, a house, a hut, a tent—is one such technology. But we've also invented some portable solutions to the same problem. There's the parasol (literally meaning to "ward off the Sun"), and of course there's that most ubiquitous of portable Sun-protectors: the hat.

Sparking Interest

- Use a collection of different hats to stimulate a class discussion about why people wear hats, and why there are so many varieties.
- Read a story about hats.
- Talk about heat- and Sun-related health concerns such as sunburns and sunstroke.

NEED

(what are we being asked to do?)

To make a hat to protect us from the sun so that:

We can play outside without getting a burn.

OR We can have a hat fashion show.

IDEAS

(what ideas do we have for doing it?)

- **What materials are available for us to work with?**

  For example:
  - paper?
  - fabrics?
  - old hats?
  - yarn?
  - cardboard?
  - ?

- **How can we keep the hat on our head when we are playing?**

  For example:
  - string?
  - elastic bands?
  - adjustable headband?
  - tight fit?
  - ?

- **How can we make the hat look nice?**

  For example:
  - paint?
  - feathers?
  - beads?
  - stickers?
  - shiny paper?
  - ?

Create
(how can we make it?)

- **What will we use to make it?**

  (Students may modify an old hat or start from scratch to make their creation. The materials that they chose will depend on their approach to the solution.)

- **How can we make sure it fits?**

  For example:
  - use an elastic band to make the headband stretchy?
  - custom fit the hat for your head?
  - tie it on with string?
  - ?

- **What tools and equipment do we need?**

  For example:
  - glue or tape?
  - markers?
  - paint?
  - scissors?
  - ?

Evaluate
(how well did we do what we needed to do?)

- **Does the hat keep the sun off our head?**
- **Is it comfortable to wear?**
- **Does it stay on when we are playing or when the wind is blowing?**
- **Could we improve it? How?**

Nicer

Invite students to design and make a parasol (umbrella) to protect them from the sun.

Family & Friends

ACTIVITY 6B:

Goodies for Grandma

For Your Interest

Gifts of food such as chocolates or cookies are a way of saying, "I Love You." The presentation of the gift is as important as the goodies that are given.

NEED
(what are we being asked to do?)

To make a container for cookies so that:

We can take them to Grandma's house.

OR We can show how important Grandma (or another special someone) is to us.

IDEAS
(what ideas do we have for doing it?)

- **What kinds of containers are there for holding cookies?**
  For example:
  – bags?
  – tins?
  – baskets?
  – ?
- **How can our container protect the cookies?**
  For example:
  – from breaking?
  – from bugs?
  – from melting?
  – ?
- **How can we make our container?**
  For example:
  – decorate an existing container?
  – make it from scratch?
  – ?

OTHER "IDEAS" OR "QUESTIONS" WE COULD THINK ABOUT

- How can we make our container easy to carry?
- How big does the container have to be to hold 1 or 2 dozen cookies?
- Which containers keep the cookies fresher?

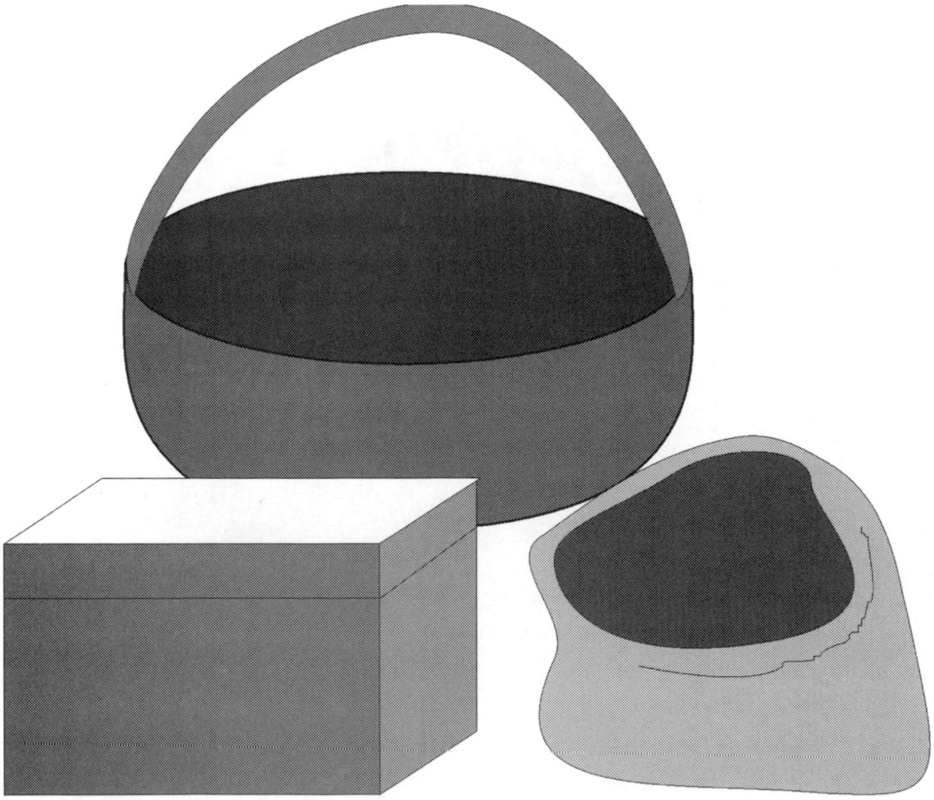

CREATE
(how can we make it?)

- **What materials would we like to use?**

  For example:
  - construction paper?
  - plastic jugs?
  - papier maché?
  - cookie tins?
  - paper bags?
  - shoe boxes?
  - ?

- **How will we decorate the container?**

  For example:
  - paint it?
  - glue on decorations?
  - put a decorative covering around it?
  - ?

- **What tools and equipment will we need?**

  For example:
  - tape?
  - glue?
  - scissors?
  - ?

EVALUATE
(how well did we do what we needed to do?)

- **Is our container big enough to hold all the cookies?**
- **Does it protect the cookies?**
- **Is it easy to carry?**
- **Could we make our container better? How?**

Nicer

Invite your students to make cookies to fill their containers.

Sparking Interest

- Read or tell the story of Little Red Riding Hood.
- Collect pictures of different types of lunch bags, boxes, and baskets.
- Have the students bring in their favourite cookie recipes, or favourite brands.

ACTIVITY 6C:

Friendship Soup

For Your Interest

Food preparation is technology in action. Pots, utensils, and measuring equipment are technological devices; peeling, cutting, and measuring of ingredients are technological processes. Preparing food is also a rich source of cross-curricular integration. For example, measuring dry and wet ingredients provides hands-on experience related to science and mathematics; noting changes in colour, texture, and flavour improve observational skills; recording kinds and amounts of ingredients involves communication skills; noting where ingredients come from (especially herbs and spices) invites opportunities for studying geography; and the act of sharing food is, historically, an ancient social tradition common virtually to all cultures around the globe.

Sparking Interest

- Read or tell the story Stone Soup.

NEED

(what are we being asked to do?)

To create a pot of Friendship Soup so that:

We can feel closer together as a class.

OR We can practice using kitchen tools and equipment safely.

OR We can practice following a recipe.*

* See Appendix 1.

IDEAS

(what ideas do we have for doing it?)

- **What kinds of ingredients does soup have?**

  For example:
  - water (or other liquids)?
  - vegetables?
  - meat?
  - herbs and spices?
  - noodles or other pasta?
  - ?

- **What tools and equipment are needed to make soup? (And what are they used for?)**

  For example:
  - pots?
  - spoons?
  - knifes?
  - measuring spoons or cups?
  - cutting board?
  - pot holders?
  - ?

- **What can we do to keep soup-making safe?**

  For example:
  - be careful when using knifes?
  - be careful around the stove burners and hot pots?
  - be careful when tasting hot soup?
  - have an adult present? wash hands before and after handling food?
  - ?

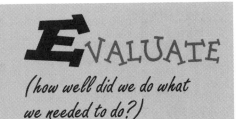

Create
(how can we make it?)

- **What ingredients do we want to use?**
  - (Depending on the time of year, ingredients may be fresh or canned or a combination of both. Any uneaten soup should be refrigerated.)
- **How can we make sure everyone has a role to play in preparing and making soup?**

  For example:
  - work in groups?
  - have different groups responsible for different jobs?
  - ?

Evaluate
(how well did we do what we needed to do?)

- **Did the soup taste good?**
- **What ingredients could we add (or take away) to make the soup better?**

Nicer

Invite the class to bring in their favourite recipes from home and publish a class cook book.

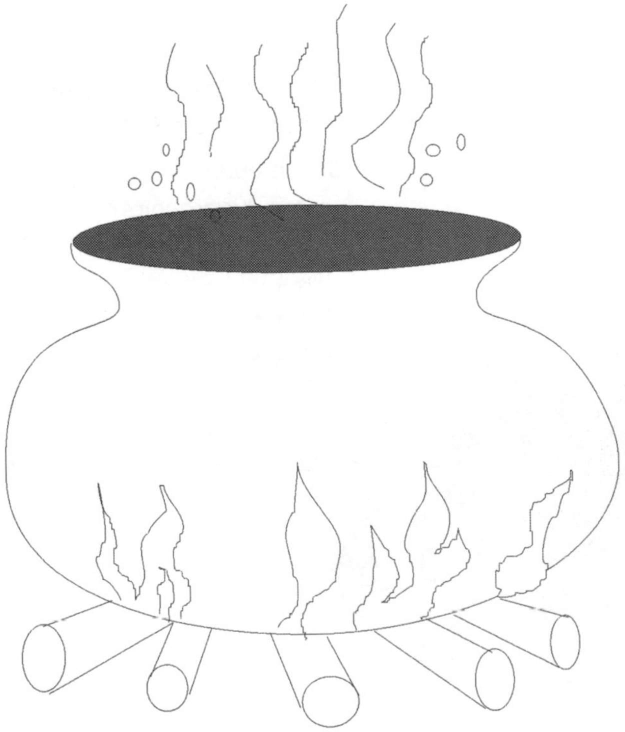

ACTIVITY 6D:

Greetings from the Heart

For Your Interest

The "ancestors" of greeting cards can be traced back to ancient Egypt, where brief messages were inscribed on scarab jewelry and given as gifts. The greeting card as we know it is a more modern innovation, originating in England and Europe during the 1800s. The first Christmas card is believed to have been made in 1843 by John Horsley, an artist. The practice of giving cards for Christmas and other special occasions spread quickly across Europe and the Americas.

Today, of course, commercial greeting cards are a booming business. For many families, however, a store-bought greeting card—no matter how attractive—can't compete with a hand-made card, especially when it comes from a daughter, son, or grandchild.

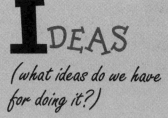

Need
(what are we being asked to do?)

To design our own, hand-made greeting card for someone special.

Ideas
(what ideas do we have for doing it?)

- **What kinds of greeting cards have we given or received?**

  For example:
  - birthday cards?
  - Mother's day/Father's Day cards?
  - get well cards?
  - religious cards?
  - Valentine's Day cards?
  - ?

- **What kinds of things do we see on greeting cards?**

  For example:
  - pictures?
  - writing (poems? riddles? jokes? sincere messages?)?
  - pop-up middles?
  - decorations (feathers? buttons? glitter? ribbon?)?
  - ?

- **How can we put words and pictures on our card?**

  For example:
  - computer graphics?
  - hand-letter and hand-draw/paint?
  - cut and paste pictures from magazines?
  - ?

Sparking Interest

- Collect and display a variety of different types of commercial greeting cards.
- Load a greeting card making program on the computer.

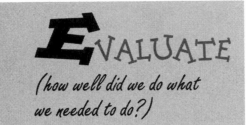

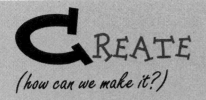

CREATE
(how can we make it?)

- **What materials do we want to use?**

  For example:
  – paper?
  – cardboard?
  – feathers?
  – shiny buttons?
  – stick-ons?
  – ?

- **What tools and equipment do we need?**

  For example:
  – scissors?
  – tape?
  – computer?
  – scanner?
  – ?

EVALUATE
(how well did we do what we needed to do?)

- **Do we like the card we made?**
- **How could we make our next card different from this one?**

Nicer

Invite students to make an envelope for their cards. You can take some commercial envelopes apart to show some pattern shapes for envelopes. Encourage students to measure carefully before they cut their pattern out. Invite the students to make their own paper for their cards. Experiment with materials such as cloth fibres, flower petals, or leaves.

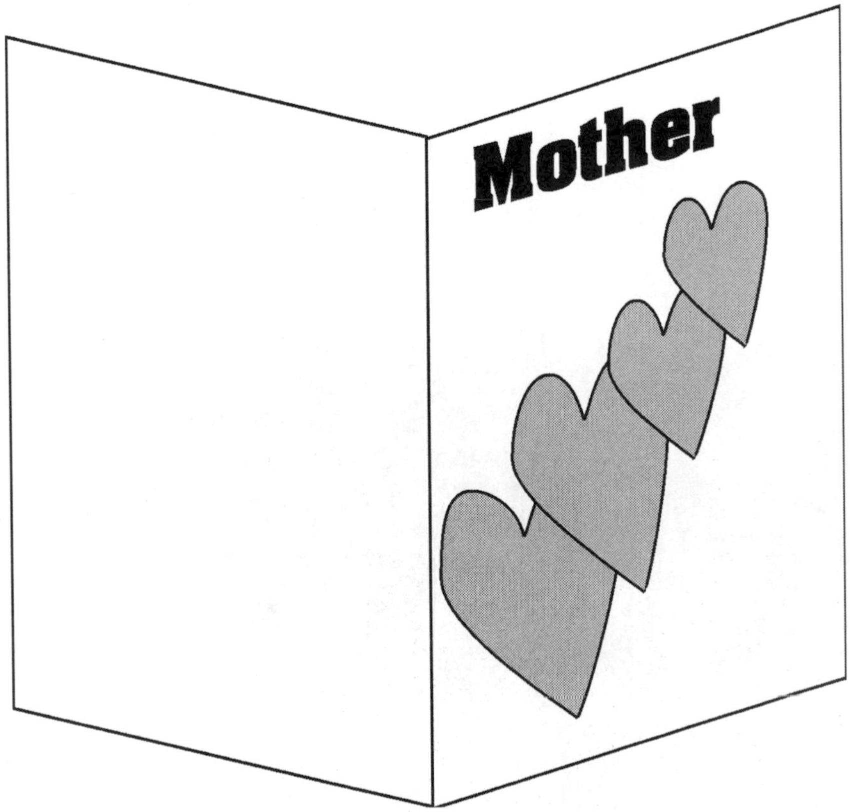

ACTIVITY 6E:

Nothing to Do?

For Your Interest

In the days before television, children had all types of games that kept them amused. They had games that could be played in fields and streets and games that could be played indoors or on the porch. Unlike video games where the rules are fixed by the designer, the rules for "kick the can", "eye spy," and many children's card games could be modified by the players to suit the occasion or the skill of the players.

Today, when students are deprived of their televisions or if the batteries for their hand-held video game die, many are at a loss for what to do. We need to ensure that we instill, for these students, the feeling that they can create their own games. Here are some ideas for doing so.

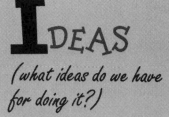

Need
(what are we being asked to do?)

To design a family game so that:

We can have something to play on a rainy day.

OR We can have something to do on a long car trip.

OR We can have something to play at the beach or when camping, etc.

Ideas
(what ideas do we have for doing it?)

- **What kind of game will we invent?**

For example:
– board game?
– puzzle game?
– card game?
– guessing game?
– ?

- **Which games need special equipment?**

For example:
– boards?
– cards?
– counters?
– scoring pads?
– game pieces?
– ?

- **What else do games need?**

For example:
– rules?
– clear instructions?
– a container?
– ?

Sparking Interest

- Collect a variety of games that students like to play.
- Sort the games into groups: board games, guessing games, puzzle games, etc.

Create
(how can we make it?)

- **What materials will we use?**

  For example:
  - pebbles?
  - buttons?
  - erasers?
  - popsicle sticks?
  - cardboard?
  - paper?
  - ?

- **What tools and equipment do we need?**

  For example:
  - ruler?
  - marker/crayon/paint?
  - pencil?
  - scissors?
  - ?

Evaluate
(how well did we do what we needed to do?)

- **Could people play the game the way we planned?**
- **Did everyone enjoy the game?**
- **Could we improve it? How?**

Nicer

Invite the students to design a container for their game. The container should hold all the parts and have the rules written on it. A picture of the game in play or how the parts are stored could be part of the container's cover.

I'm BORED!
When are we going to get there?

ACTIVITY 6F:

Try Puppetry

For Your Interest

Puppets have been used for entertainment and education for hundreds of years. The smallest and simplest puppets are finger puppets. The four most common types of puppets are hand or glove puppets, rod puppets, marionettes, and shadow puppets. The best-known glove puppet is probably Lambchop, made famous by Sherri Lewis. Rod puppets are the type used frequently by Jim Henson and his group. Marionettes, like Pinocchio, are string puppets. Shadow puppets came from ancient China. They are two-dimensional cutouts which are operated by rods or strings. They are illuminated from behind, and the audience sees only the shadow profile of the puppet.

NEED (what are we being asked to do?)

To make a puppet so that:

We can do a puppet show.
OR We can entertain another class.

IDEAS (what ideas do we have for doing it?)

- **What type of puppets could we make?**

  For example:
  – hand puppets?
  – marionettes?
  – stick puppets?
  – finger puppets?
  – ?

- **What materials could we use?**

  For example:
  – wood?
  – cloth?
  – paper?
  – yarn?
  – string?
  – papier maché?
  – ?

- **What characters will the puppets be?**

  For example:
  – boys and girls?
  – animals?
  – monsters?
  – fairies?
  – ?

Sparking Interest

- Display a variety of puppets (or pictures of puppets).
- Show video clips of different TV puppet characters.
- Read a story involving a puppet character.

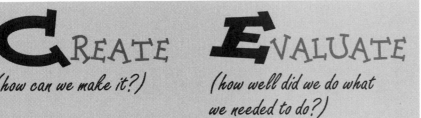

CREATE
(how can we make it?)

- **What materials and equipment do we need if we make a finger puppet:**
  For example:
  – coloured paper?
  – scissors?
  – glue or tape?
  – ?
- **make a hand puppet?**
  For example:
  – an old glove or sock?
  – buttons?
  – scraps of yarn?
  – ?
- **make a marionette?**
  For example:
  – wood?
  – string?
  – cardboard tubes and containers?
  – old plastic containers?
  – paint?
  – ?
- **make a shadow puppet?**
  For example:
  – dark paper?
  – scissors?
  – wood?
  – ?

EVALUATE
(how well did we do what we needed to do?)

- **Does the puppet work the way we planned?**
- **How is it different from others made in our class?**
- **Could we make it better? How?**

Nicer

Invite the students to make a puppet theatre in which they can put on a show.

PLEASE SAVE ME!

A Note to Parents/Guardians

Dear Parent/Guardian

Our children are doing some exciting projects in art, science, and technology. Please help us by saving the following items for use at school.

- ❑ Styrofoam
  - ❑ meat trays
  - ❑ cups
  - ❑ packing chips
- ❑ Aluminum
  - ❑ pie tins
  - ❑ TV dinner trays
  - ❑ foil
- ❑ Clothes pins
  - ❑ snap
  - ❑ peg
- ❑ Wallpaper pieces
- ❑ Fabric scraps
  - ❑ felt
  - ❑ cotton
  - ❑ cotton/polyester
  - ❑ burlap
  - ❑ velvet
- ❑ Yarn
- ❑ Empty tin cans
  - ❑ soup
  - ❑ pop
  - ❑ juice
- ❑ Magazines
- ❑ Egg crates
- ❑ Trims such as
  - ❑ lace
  - ❑ buttons
  - ❑ ribbon
- ❑ Gift wrap scraps
- ❑ Cardboard tubes from
  - ❑ foil
  - ❑ waxed paper
  - ❑ paper towel
  - ❑ wrapping paper
- ❑ Plastic bottles
  - ❑ dish detergent
  - ❑ mouthwash
  - ❑ soda pop
- ❑ Wire coat hangers
- ❑ Old spools
  - ❑ thread
  - ❑ fishing line
  - ❑ ribbon
- ❑ Clean old socks
- ❑ Lids from
  - ❑ jam jars
  - ❑ pickle jars
  - ❑ juice bottles
- ❑ Natural materials
  - ❑ pine cones
  - ❑ acrons
  - ❑ feathers
  - ❑ shells
  - ❑ rocks
- ❑ Hardware
  - ❑ old keys
  - ❑ nails
  - ❑ bolts
  - ❑ nuts
  - ❑ washers
- ❑ Junk jewellery
- ❑ Old toys
  - ❑ clockwork or
  - ❑ electric motor powered
- ❑ Broken appliances
  - ❑ toasters
  - ❑ radios
  - ❑ electric drills

Thank you for your help.

ADDITIONAL EQUIPMENT YOU CAN MAKE

The Bench Hook

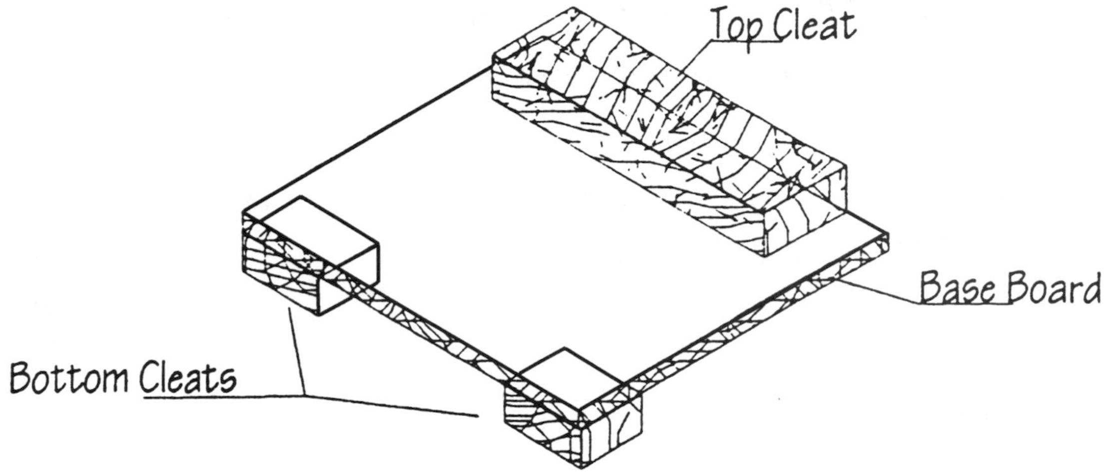

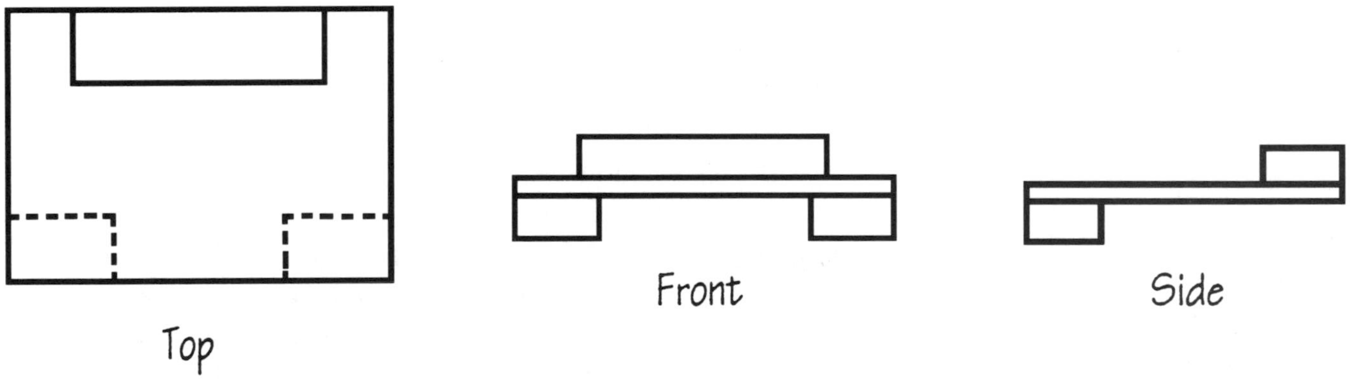

Bench hooks are devices used to protect tables while cutting wood or other materials with a saw.

They also help the user to hold the material steady while cutting.

A bench hook is made from scrap lumber. The dimensions are not critical.

The base board should be about 20 cm x 15 cm. It is made from plywood (10–20 mm thick) or hardwood (12–20 mm thick). The top and bottom cleats are made from 1 x 2 nominal stapping.

The top cleat is approximately 10 cm shorter than the width of the baseboard and is centred on the baseboard. This provides a 5 cm wide cutting area on either end for left or right handed students. All cleats are glued and nailed to the baseboard.

By using two small pieces for the bottom cleats, the bench hook can be used on round tables and still provide steady support.

▶ Appendix 3

Recipes for Pioneer Cooking

Sour Dough Starter

500 ml	all purpose flour
25 ml	sugar
500 ml	warm water

Mix ingredients in a large bowl and cover with a clean tea towel. Let stand in a warm area of the room for 2–3 days. When it is spongy and develops a yeasty aroma it is ready. Keep covered in a refrigerator or freeze in an air tight container.

The starter must be fed once a week when it is thawed. Feed by stirring in 250 ml milk and 50 ml sugar.

Oatmeal Bread

500 ml	sifted all purpose flour
5 ml	salt
5 ml	baking powder
80 ml	white sugar
5 ml	baking soda
500 ml	rolled oats
125 ml	molasses
30 ml	melted shortening
500 ml	sour milk
250 ml	raisins or dates

Sift first 5 ingredients together. Add oats, molasses, melted shortening and milk. Mix thoroughly and add fruit. Pour into a greased loaf pan. Let it set 20 minutes then bake for 1 hour at 180°C.

Sour Dough Bread

250 ml	sour dough starter
1.4 l	milk
125 ml	sugar
25 ml	salt
60 ml	molasses
2	eggs
170 g	melted shortening OR 115 g lard
1 kg	white flour
800 g	whole wheat flour

Mix milk, sugar and salt in a large bowl. Beat in eggs. Mix in molasses and shortening. Add starter. Stir in white flour and beat until smooth. Mix in remaining flour and knead until dough forms a smooth ball. Place in a greased bowl and cover. Allow to rise for about two hours until double in bulk.

Grease 4 bread pans. Punch down and knead. Divide into eight equal pieces. Knead each piece until all air bubbles are gone. Place two pieces in each pan. Set aside to rise until double in bulk (2 hr.)

Bake at 200°C for 10 minutes and reduce the heat to 180°C for a further 30 min. Break loaves apart to be sure they are fully cooked.

Recipes for Pioneer Cooking

Quick Whole Wheat Corn Bread

250 ml	corn meal
250 ml	whole wheat flour
30 ml	sugar
2.5 ml	salt
250 ml	milk
60 ml	vegetable oil
1	egg

In a large bowl combine corn meal, flour, sugar, baking powder, and salt. Set aside. In a small bowl combine egg, oil and milk. Add this to flour mixture and blend lightly. Bake in a greased loaf pan at 220°C for 20–25 minutes. Cut in squares and serve hot.

Country Spoon Bread

250 ml	corn meal
750 ml	milk
5 ml	salt
5 ml	baking powder
30 ml	melted butter
3	egg yolks, beaten
3	egg whites, stiffly beaten

Cook corn meal in 500 ml of milk for 10 minutes or until it attains a porridge like consistency. Away from heat, add salt, baking powder, butter and remaining milk. Add egg yolks and blend well. Fold in egg whites. Bake in bowl in a slow oven (120°C) for 1 hour. Serve spooned onto warm plates and topped with butter.

Indian Griddle Cakes

500 ml	Indian (corn) meal
250 ml	flour
	pinch of salt
	ginger
15 ml	molasses
5 ml	baking soda
	sour milk as required

Mix all ingredients into a thick batter. Pour onto a hot greased griddle or fry pan. Fry until brown, turn and fry other side.

Sugar Cookies

125 ml	soft shortening
60 ml	butter or margarine
2	eggs, beaten
2.5 ml	vanilla
625 ml	flour
5 ml	salt
5 ml	baking powder

Combine shortening butter, eggs and vanilla. Add flour, salt and baking powder. Mix thoroughly. Chill the dough for 1 hour and then roll out thinly. Cut into shapes and bake sprinkled with sugar on an ungreased cookie sheet at 210°C for 6–8 minutes.

Appendix 3

RECIPES FOR PIONEER COOKING

Currant and Raspberry Jam

450 g	red currants
100 g	raspberries
550 g	sugar

Place fruit into saucepan and add sugar. Bring to a boil and stir. Boil for ¾ of an hour after mixture boils. Put jam in sterilized preserving jars or eat quickly (when cool).

Strawberry Jam

450 g	strawberries
450 g	sugar

Bring to a boil and stir while boiling for 25 minutes. Pour into sterilized preserving jars or eat quickly (when cool).

Ginger Snaps

30 ml	water
125 ml	molasses
45 ml	butter
250 ml	flour
2.5 ml	baking soda
30 ml	ginger
1.2 ml	cinnamon
80 ml	sugar
	pinch of salt
1.2 ml	nutmeg

Bring water, molasses and butter to a boil. Cool. Sift together remaining ingredients and add to molasses mixture. Stir well. Roll out to 4 mm thick. Cut into shapes and bake at 180°C for 5–8 minutes.

Recipe for Friendship Soup

Friendship soup is a vegetable soup which can be made from any fresh vegetables. The following recipe is a guide to suggest some possible ingredients.

In a large stock pot combine the following ingredients:

3 l	water
8	bullion cubes or 4 cans consommé
500 ml	diced carrots
150 ml	diced parsnip
3	large onions, chopped fine
250 ml	diced celery
1	large leek, sliced thin
5	large tomatoes, sliced
5 ml	savory
2.5 ml	marjoram
1.2 ml	dill seed
5 ml	dry mustard
2.5 ml	peppercorns
30 ml	coarse salt
15 ml	sugar
150 ml	barley

Bring to a boil. Cover and simmer for 2–3 hours stirring occasionally.

APPROACHES TO ASSESSMENT

As students experience opportunities to complete application challenges, we must include an assessment of the observations we make of their **process** of learning as well as the **products** of their efforts. Whether they are conducting experiments, making representative simulations, or assembling a product, we need to assess the acquisition of a new set of skills. By observing the process of learning, we will assess creative thinking, inquiry and problem solving, and the development of appropriate attitudes.

Assumptions

Before developing assessment strategies, some basic assumptions need to be made:

1. Although strategies for assessing challenges are necessary elements in the teaching-learning process, there is **no single assessment vehicle that will provide a complete profile of the learner;**
2. Assessment must be learner-focused. Whatever assessment strategies we generate, they must have the ability to assess students **as they learn** and **how they learn;**
3. Learning is an integrating experience. Throughout the process of learning, we must take every opportunity to **point to the connections with other parts of the student's curriculum.**

Choosing an Assessment Strategy

It will be advantageous for us to choose one assessment strategy, or components of several strategies that will work best for the student activity.

Factors in our decision will include:

3. the nature of the challenge being assessed;
4. whether or not the strategy allows an assessment of a broad range of skills and behaviors;
5. the time it will take to conduct the chosen strategy.

Checklists

Throughout the assessment process, we will be aware that students are supplying us with evidences of their developmental processes, thoughts and actions. It is essential for students to be aware that we will be observing these and that they will be supplying us with these evidences. As we ask students to account for their reasoning or verbal descriptions of events that are happening, we will need to capture these imaginative thoughts and actions in some way. This recognizes students as active participants and in many instances, can be a motivation for them to improve these evidences.

The use of a Checklist with a set of "prompting" questions can assist in giving us evidence of the judgments students are making about their own observations, understandings, and actions.

Types of prompting questions could include:

6. **Descriptive word lists:** sets of word prompts where students make judgments about their observations;
7. **Teacher/student interactions:** questions we can ask students to gain insight into their understanding and involvement with the activity;
8. **Teacher observations:** questions we can ask ourselves about our perceptions of the understanding and involvement of each student with the activity.

Appendix 4

Prompting questions using **Descriptive Word Lists:**

The "Prompting" questions offered as examples below are suitable for early grades and for an activity involving a judgment of materials used in the activity. Word lists will need to be tailored to the grade and application challenge.

Word Lists

Activity ____________________ **Name** ___________________________

Are the materials you are using:

• bright	colourful	glossy	dull
• smooth	fuzzy	coarse	rough
• soft	fluffy	hard	brittle
• impressive	neat	attractive	ugly
• strong	durable	flexible	weak
• light	puffy	bulky	heavy

Summary Comments

Although the word list above can help us assess a student's judgments about the materials they are using, the list can also assist in making connections to other parts of the curriculum. In this example, the checklist can be used to increase word power or to build a vocabulary of terms. Over time, students should be encouraged to move beyond simple yes/no answers to responses that are closer to complete sentences.

Prompting questions using **Teacher/student Interactions:**

The following is a representative set of prompting questions that we can ask students to help us assess the **process of learning** as it is taking place and some judgments about the **product of their actions**. Since it is impossible to observe everything that is happening in an activity-based environment, we must focus and limit our observations to a manageable set.

Teacher/Student Interactions

Activity ______________________ **Name** ______________________

PROCESS: **Specific Comments**

- Did you understand the challenge? ______________
- What ideas did you contribute? ______________
- What did others think of your idea? ______________
- Did others have good ideas? ______________
- Why was this idea/solution chosen? ______________
- What procedure/materials did you choose to use? Why? ______________
- What part of the challenge will you/did you work on? ______________
- Did you help others with their part in the challenge? ______________
- Did you have any difficulties with your part in the challenge? ______________

PRODUCT:

- Did your product solve what you set out to achieve in the challenge?
- Were there other materials/procedures you might have used?
- Was your product safe to use?
- Can your product be used, or modified to be used, for anything else?

Summary Comments

____

____

____

Appendix 4

Prompting questions using **Teacher Observations:**

The following is a set of questions we can ask ourselves as passive observers or through interactions with our students.

Teacher Observations

Activity ______________________ **Name** ______________________

Does the student: **Specific Comments**

- have the ability to describe the challenge? ______________
- take part in group discussions? ______________
- share ideas and information? ______________
- make suggestions? ______________
- listen to others suggestions? ______________
- participate well in the activity? ______________
- cooperate well with others? ______________
- show enthusiasm and motivation for the challenge? ______________
- experiment with different materials? ______________
- use tools and materials appropriately? ______________

Summary Comments

____

____

____

____

____

____

____

____

RATING SCALES (RUBRICS)

Where checklists make either/or judgments about whether or not a student is moving toward a standard of achievement, Rating Scales make judgments about the intensity (how good? how often?) of the achievement. Rating scales are particularly helpful in assessing behaviours; what we see a student do or hear the student say. They can also be of value in assessing a specific skill, performance, procedure, ability, or product. Rating scales assume all students will exhibit skills and behaviours in varying amounts or at different rates to a predetermined observation criteria. Rating Scales can be applied not only to the process and product of an activity-rich environment, but also to other areas of the curriculum.

Rating Scales with **descriptive categories** not only give us insights into the "process" the student is using but also gives us evidences where support or remediation may be appropriate. Achievements on these rating scales may also provide evidence that the student can be challenged beyond the criteria chosen.

The descriptive categories in the following rating scales are examples only. Teachers should develop descriptors that truly reflect the evidences that would be appropriate to the specific activity.

Appendix 4

Ratings with Descriptive Categories: Assesses the degree of achievement.

Process of Learning

Activity ______________________ **Name** ______________________

1. Has the ability to describe the challenge.
   N/A Not at all In a small way To some extent To a great extent

2. Takes part in group discussions.
   N/A Never Seldom Sometimes Often Always

3. Shares ideas and information.
   N/A Never Seldom Sometimes Often Always

4. Makes suggestions.
   N/A Never Seldom Sometimes Often Always

5. Listens to others suggestions.
   N/A Never Seldom Sometimes Often Always

6. Participates well in the activity.
   N/A Never Seldom Sometimes Often Always

7. Cooperates well with others.
   N/A Never Seldom Sometimes Often Always

8. Shows enthusiasm and motivation for the challenge.
   N/A Not at all In a small way To some extent To a great extent

9. Uses equipment and materials appropriately.
   N/A Never Seldom Sometimes Often Always

Summary Comments

____

____

____

____

Scored Rating Scales: This scale uses numerical values to assess the "quality" of a student's performance or the product of the activity. This method asks us to select a numerical value that best describes that quality. When numerical values of 1 to 5 are used for example, we should attempt to design a descriptive criteria that truly reflects the numerical value given to it.

Scored Rating Scale

Activity ______________________ **Name** ______________________

Scale:
0 = N/A—not enough information to judge or has not had an opportunity to apply the criteria.
1 = Needs improvement—exhibits minimal effort.
2 = Not up to expectations—has not achieved minimal expectations.
3 = Good effort—reasonable attempt to achieve expectations.
4 = Excellent effort—achieves all expectations.
5 = Outstanding effort—achieves beyond expectations and is a mentor to others.

Criteria	**Scale**
1. has the ability to describe the challenge.	0 1 2 3 4 5
2. takes part in group discussions.	0 1 2 3 4 5
3. shares ideas and information.	0 1 2 3 4 5
4. makes suggestions.	0 1 2 3 4 5
5. listens to others suggestions.	0 1 2 3 4 5
6. participates well in the activity.	0 1 2 3 4 5
7. cooperates well with others.	0 1 2 3 4 5
8. shows enthusiasm and motivation for the challenge.	0 1 2 3 4 5
9. experiments with different materials.	0 1 2 3 4 5
10. uses tools and materials appropriately.	0 1 2 3 4 5

Total Score: ____________
50

Summary Comments

____

____

▶ Appendix 4

In Summary:

When developing assessment strategies, we must consider the following:

- No single assessment vehicle will give a complete profile of the learner.
- Strategies must be learner focused.
- Where possible, connections must be made to other parts of the curriculum.
- Constructing Checklists and Rating Scales take time, but systematic observation of students can be a most effective tool for a comprehensive assessment as well as providing the foundation for discussions with our students, their parents, and other staff.
- Developing criteria for observation skills will improve over time and with practice.
- Select one or two types of skills or behaviors to observe at one time.
- Limit observations to a few students at a time.
- Assessing an activity-based program is not substantially different from assessment in other parts of the curriculum.

IDEAS AND TECHNIQUES

The following resources are practical in nature and introduce teachers and children to the ideas, materials and techniques required to design and make things.

Caney, Steven; *Steven Caney's Invention Book,* Workman Publishing Co. Inc., 1985.
ISBN 0-89480-076-0
Explains the steps of the process of becoming an inventor. Has stories that tell the history of inventions we commonly know about. Also has a few start-up ideas or inspirations in a list of Fantasy Inventions that follow each story.

Catherall, Ed and Bev McKay; *Turning to Wheels,* Chrysalis Publications, 1988.
ISBN 0-921049-13-7
Reproducible activity pages of simple projects using wheels in more than 30 applications.

Dalzell, Rosie; *We Can Join It,* Cherrytree Press Ltd., 1991.
ISBN 0-7451-5128-0
From the making of glue through paper folding, sewing, knotting, taping, and weaving, children learn how to use simple materials to make things.

Dalzell, Rosie; *We Can Move It,* Cherrytree Press Ltd., 1991.
ISBN 0-7451-5129-9
Centred around the theme of "moving things", children are introduced, through project applications, to rollers, trolleys, sliders, magnets, balloons, and pivots.

Gadd, Tim and Dianne Morton; *Technology Key Stage 1,* Stanley Thornes Ltd., 1992.
Distributed in Canada through Bacon and Hughes.
ISBN 0-7487-1357-3
Huge bank of ideas, activities, and photocopiable sheets. Demonstrates how technology can be introduced through themes and topics, stories and challenges. Also includes techniques and resources for record keeping and assessment.

Gadd, Tim and Dianne Morton; *Technology Key Stage 2,* Stanley Thornes Ltd., 1992.
Distributed in Canada through Bacon and Hughes.
ISBN 0-7487-1495-2
Additional bank of ideas, activities, and photocopiable sheets. Demonstrates how technology can be introduced through themes and topics, stories and challenges. Also includes techniques and resources for record keeping and assessment.

Harrison, Patricia and Chris Ryan, *Technology in Action: Unit 1,* Folens Ltd.,1990.
ISBN 1-85276115-6
A binder of activity sheets and teacher's resource booklet that introduces the topics of Ourselves, The Farm, Homes and Toys. Each topic has several activities or challenges on laminated sheets. The supporting teacher resource also has an excellent section on using simple materials to develop basic skills.

Great Resources

Harrison, Patricia and Chris Ryan; *Technology in Action: Unit 2,* Folens Ltd.,1990.
ISBN 1-85276116-4
Same structure and resources as Technology in Action: Unit 1. The topics in this unit include Vehicles, Creatures, School, and The Park.

Horvatic, Anne; *Simple machines,* E. P. Dutton: New York; Fitzhenry and Whiteside, 1989.
ISBN 0-525-44492-0
A well illustrated picture book of simple machines used in places you might never expect. Everyday examples of the wheel, inclined plane, wedge, screw and lever are described.

Kerrod, Robin; *How Things Work,* Marshall Cavendish Corp., 1990.
ISBN 1-85435-154-0
Several well-illustrated and easy to follow pages of project ideas and how they work. Projects ranging from flight and simple propulsion to the making of electricity with a lemon, use simple and commonly available materials.

Knapp, Brian; *How Things Work,* Grolier Ltd., 1991.
ISBN 0-7172-2783-9
From a tap works to a vacuum cleaner, this book plots a structural path of science, design, and technology.

Lampton, Christopher; *Seesaws, Nutcrackers and Brooms,* Millbrook Press, 1991.
ISBN 1-878841-43-2
An illustrated picture book describing simple machines that are really levers.

Malam, John; *Pop-up Machines,* Alfred A. Knopf Inc., 1991.
ISBN 0-679-80872-8
Five of today's strongest machines come to life off the pages. These pop-ups are contrasted with the way things used to be in the past.

Metro Toronto School Board Teachers; All Aboard! Cross-Curricular Design and Technology Strategies and Activities, Trifolium Books Inc., 1996.
ISBN 1-895579-86-4
Shows how design and technology can be integrated in every elementary classroom and explains how to use problem-solving skills creatively. 50 activities.

Reynolds, Bill and Bob Corney and Norm Dale; *Technology IDEAS,* Prentice-Hall Inc., 1993.
ISBN 0-02-954154-9
Excellent for late primary grades, this teacher resource uses an open-ended problem solving process and is designed to assist teachers in directing children to solve challenges organized in thematic units. A Useful tools/techniques section.

Richards, Roy; *An Early Start To Technology,* Simon & Schuster Inc.,1990.
ISBN 0-7501-0033-8
A well illustrated and described gathering of experiences that make close links

to technology and science. Provided is a wealth of practical experiences that will involve children in looking at structures, materials, forces, energy, and how things are controlled.

Rockwell, Anne; *Machines,* Macmillan Publishing, 1972.
ISBN 0-02-777520-8
Illustrations and descriptions of everyday machines that make work easier.

Sellwood, Peter and Fred Ward and Ron Lewin; *Let's Make It Work,* MacMillan Education Ltd., 1990.
ISBN 0-333-44023-4
This Introductory Book introduces children to simple technology and science through a problem solving approach. Concepts and skills are systematically developed through simple work with different materials.

Stroud, Peter; *Tools,* Cherrytree Press Ltd., 1991.
ISBN 0-7451-5148-5
A storybook introducing recognizable tools that help us do things that we cannot do with our bare hands.

Williams, John; *First Technology: Tools,* Wayland Publishers Ltd.,1993.
ISBN 0-7502-0650-0
A paper streamer activity enables children to use some basic tools that are clearly described and illustrated.

Williams, John; *Starting Technology: Machines,* Wayland Publishers Ltd.,1991.
ISBN 0-7502-0025-1
A book of creative ideas for making levers, diggers, cranes, pulleys and switches. The making of models support an understanding of how machines work.

Williams, John; *Starting Technology: Wheels,* Wayland Publishers Ltd.,1990.
ISBN 0-7502-0271-8
A book of creative ideas to make rollers, carts, trolleys, gears, and waterwheels to find out about movement.

Williams, Peter and Jacobson, Saryl; *Take a Technowalk to Learn About Materials and Structures*, Trifolium Books Inc., 1997.
ISBN 1-895579-76-7
Shows how to take students on 10 neighbourhood Technowalks to learn about materials and structures.

Zubrowski, Bernie; *Messing Around With Drinking Straw Construction,* Little, Brown and Co., 1981.
ISBN 0-316-98873-1
Directions for the making of drinking straw models to explore how houses, bridges and towers are made.

COMMUNITIES

Bourgeois, Paulette and Kim LaFave; *Canadian Fire Fighters,* Kids Can Press, 1991.
ISBN 1-55074-042-3
Lively verses and illustrations tell the story of an hour in a small boy's life one hectic Monday morning.

Bourgeois, Paulette and Kim Lafave; *Canadian Garbage Collectors,* Kids Can Press, 1991.
ISBN 1-55074-040-7
An illustrated depiction of a day in the life of a garbage collector and highlighting the 3 Rs of Reduce, Reuse, and Recycle.

Bourgeois, Paulette and Kim LaFave; *Canadian Postal Workers,* Kids Can Press, 1992.
ISBN 1-55074-058-X
This illustrated book traces the route of a letter written by a child to his Grandmother thousands of miles away. It also depicts a day in the life of a postal worker.

Cobb, Vicki; *Skyscraper Going Up!* Harper and Row Publishers Inc., 1987.
ISBN 0-690-04525-5
A pop-up book showing the "bones", "heart", "skin", and "lungs" of a building. Children can be the builders with bright, colourful paper mechanics guiding their participation.

Corcos, Lucille; *The City Book,* Western Publishing Co., 1972.
ISBN 0-307-65772-8
Watercolour illustrations and descriptions about cities and all the things that happen when people come together to build their homes, stores, and markets and to make and trade the things they make things they needed.

Gibbons, Gail; *Up Goes The Skyscraper!* Four Winds Press: Macmillan Publishing Co., 1986
ISBN 0-02-736780-0
A clearly described and colourful construction of a skyscraper. Playing the part of people on the street, children can see it rise before their eyes.

Green, John F.; *Junk Pile Jennifer,* Scholastic Inc., 1991.
ISBN 0-590-73680-9
A visual experience with Jennifer who loves junk. The neighbourhhood thinks she is crazy as she looks for new treasures to build a cosy house in the backyard.

Hoban, Tana; *Dig, Drill, Dump, Fill,* Greenwillow Books, 1975.
ISBN 0-688-80016-5
Photographs help children use their eyes and minds imaginatively with heavy machinery.

Jeunesse, Gallimard and Claude Delafosse; *On Wheels,* Moonlight Publishing Ltd., 1991.
ISBN 1-85103-111-1

A ride in a car, fire engine, racing car, ambulance, bulldozer, bicycle, and bus takes you on a trip through the sights and sounds of the city and countryside.

Rockwell, Harlow; *My Dentist,* Greenwillow Books, 1975.
ISBN 0-688-80004-1
Economic text combined with colourful illustrations of dentist office procedures and equipment.

Rockwell, Harlow; *My Doctor,* Macmillan Publishing Company Inc., 1973.
ISBN 0-02-777480-5
A picture book with short effective descriptions of the doctor's office and the medical equipment used.

Pfanner, Louise; *Louise Builds A House,* Orchard Books, 1989.
ISBN 0-531-05769-8
A pattern of simple words and absorbing pictures to satisfy any child who has ever longed to create a wonderful dream house. Louise's house appears page by page and piece by piece in imaginative detail.

Shefelman, Janice; *Victoria House,* Gulliver Books: Harcourt Brace Jovanovich, 1988.
ISBN 0-15-200630-3
A story with pictures of an old Victorian house moved from the country to its new location on a city street, where a family fixes it up and moves in.

Wilson, Forrest; *What It Feels Like To Be A Building,* The Preservation Press, 1988.
ISBN 0-89133-147-6
In simple and direct explanations and with lively drawings, children will find out about architecture. They will learn how they would feel if they were squashed, pushed, shoved, and tugged at, just as the parts of buildings are.

FAMILY & FRIENDS

Franklyn, Mary Eliza; *Pepper Makes Me Sneeze,* Petheric Press Ltd., 1978.
ISBN 0-919380-25-5
The junior chef is led through some interesting bits of Nova Scotia and with some helpful hints and reminders about what preparing food is all about.

Hughes, Shirley; *Moving Molly,* The Bodley Head Ltd., 1984.
ISBN 0-370-30125-0
A story about Molly and her family and the ordeals of moving.

Smith, Lucia B.; *My Mom Got A Job,* Holt, Rinehart and Winston, 1979.
ISBN 0-03-048321-2

Special times and days spent with mother are gone when mom goes to work. Some changes in life are fun and bring a new meaning to the whole family.

Stevenson, James; *The Sea View Hotel,* Greenwillow Books, 1978.
ISBN 0-688-80168-4
A skillfully paced read-aloud about a whopping tale concocted by Grandpa.

Spier, Peter; *Oh Were They Ever Happy,* Doubleday and Company Inc., 1978
ISBN 0-385-13175-5
Resourceful children and one great idea, turn an unsupervised Saturday into a bedlam of paints, brushes, and pets underfoot.

Super, Gretchen; *What Kind Of Family Do You Have?* Twenty First Century Books, 1991.
ISBN 0-941477-64-9
A look at families like yours, unlike yours and families that are as different as the people who live in them.

PIONEERING

Adams, Peter; *Early Loggers And The Sawmill,* Crabtree Publishing Co., 1981.
ISBN 0-86505-006-6
An excellent set of early photographs and artist's illustrations with descriptions of early settlers and their logging and sawing operations.

Anno, Mitsumasa; *The Earth Is A Sundial,* The Bodley Head Ltd., 1984
ISBN 0-370-31016-0
A pop-up book with activities designed to use shadows to tell time.

Gibbons, Gail; *Farming,* Holiday House Inc., 1988.
ISBN 0-8234-0682-2
A picture book describing the activities and special qualities of life on the farm.

Gibbons, Gail; *The Milk Makers,* Macmillan Publishing Co., 1985.
ISBN 0-02-736640-5
Beginning with the cow, production, transportation, processing and final delivery of milk to the store is illustrated.

Goldreich, Gloria, Ester Goldreich and Robert Ipcar; *What Can She Be?—A Farmer,* Lothrop, Lee and Shepard Co., 1976.
ISBN 0-688-41768-X
The joys and satisfactions, as well as the hard work of running a farm, are conveyed in clear, simple language and photo-examples. Two farming sisters are followed through the changing seasons on a busy farm.

Greenwood, Barbara; *A Pioneer Story,* Kids Can Press Ltd., 1994.
ISBN 1-55074-237-X
A story of a pioneer family living on a backwoods farm in 1840. Following the family through the year until winter closes around them, children will learn what it is like to attend a backwoods school, weave cloth, and build a house.

Greenwood, Barbara; *Pioneer Crafts,* Kids Can Press Ltd., 1997.
ISBN 1-55074-359-7
Illustrated step-by-step instructions to make crafts the same way pioneer children did. Crafts include making a rag doll, silhouette portrait, spatter stenciling, crazy quilt, moccasins, and candle making.

Humphrey, Henry; *The Farm,* Doubleday and Co., 1978.
ISBN 0-385-01388-4
A photographic picture book helps children find out what a real farm is all about. Clear, simple text gives a realistic snapshot of contemporary farm life.

Kalman, Bobbie; *Early Schools,* Crabtree Publishing Co., 1982.
ISBN 0-86505-014-7
Education, because of the work that had to be done, was for a time, a luxury the early settler could not afford. The book traces these early hardships, the school day and the consequences children faced.

Kalman, Bobbie; *Early Stores And Markets,* Crabtree Publishing Co., 1981.
ISBN 0-86505-004-X
A collection of photographs and artist's illustrations depicting life with the Trading Post and 17th and 18th Century store. Described are the many professions of the storekeeper, the goods sold, and the barter system.

Kalman, Bobbie; *Early Travel,* Crabtree Publishing Co., 1981.
ISBN 0-86505-008-2
This book traces why early settlers had to travel, the means used, and the conditions they faced.

Kalman, Bobbie; *Early Village Life,* Crabtree Publishing Co., 1981.
ISBN 0-86505-010-4
A collection of photographs and artist's illustrations traces an odyssey of life in the backwoods. Depicted are earliest examples of people sharing resources, working together, while also having a good time.

Kalman, Bobbie; *Food For The Settler,* Crabtree Publishing Co., 1982.
ISBN 0-86505-012-0
Beginning with the first pioneers in the bush, the book traces the early growing of crops, raising animals, preparing dinners, and the making of bread and butter.

SPACE

Bantock, Nick; *Wings: A Pop-Up Book Of Things That Fly,* Random House, 1990.
ISBN 0-679-81041-2
Spectacular three-dimensional pop-ups and pull-tabs show children how wings really work on everything from bats and dragonflies to fighter planes and supersonic jets.

Catherall, Ed.; *Dropping In On Gravity,* Chrysalis Publications, 1988.
ISBN 0-921049-14-5
Pages of reproduceable activities that range from the making of a mobile to a game to launch a satellite, all support an understanding of the forces of gravity.

Cole, Joanna; *The Magic School Bus; Lost In The Solar System,* Scholastic Inc., 1990.
ISBN 0-590-41429-1
Blast off with Ms. Frizzle and her bus load of children on a field trip to the solar system.

Dixon, Malcolm; *Flight,* Wayland Publishers Ltd., 1990.
ISBN 1-85210-931-9
From dandelion seeds and natures flight technology and hot-air balloons to rocket-propelled spacecraft, this book explains the technology behind many forms of flight. Activities are used throughout to support an understanding of these forms.

Francis, Neil; *Super Fliers,* Kids Can Press Ltd., 1988.
ISBN 0-921103-37-9
A book beginning with discovering how flying fish and squirrels fly to the many mysteries of flight. Instructions are included to make and fly paper airplanes, helicopters, kites, parachutes, gliders, and more.

Little, Kate; *Things That Fly,* Usborne Publishing Ltd., 1987.
ISBN 1-85123-204-4
Colourfully illustrated explanations of how the first fliers to the worlds biggest and fastest planes stay up in the air.

Mackie, Dan; *Flight,* Hayes Publishing Ltd., 1986.
ISBN 0-88625-112-5
Ideal for later primary grades in giving children an overlook of many sides of flight.

Mackie, Dan; *Space Tour,* Hayes Publishing Ltd., 1986.
ISBN 0-88625-103-6
Ideal for later primary grades in giving children an opportunity to imagine they will be preparing for spaceflight.

Morris, Campbell; *Advanced Paper Aircraft Construction,* Angus and Robertson Publishers, 1989.
ISBN 0-207-14502-4
Easy to follow folding and throwing instructions for 14 darts, gliders and spinners.

Myring, Lynn; *Finding Out About Rockets And Spaceflight,* Usborne Publishing Ltd., 1982.
ISBN 0-86020-584-3
A picture information book that will answer many questions asked by children who are discovering the mysteries of space and space travel. Answers are given to such questions as; why do astronauts wear space suits?; can people live in space?; how do rockets work?; and what is a satellite?

Petty, Kate; *On A Plane,* Aladdin Books Ltd./Franklin Watts, 1984.
ISBN 0-531-04716-4
Full colour art work and large easy-to-read text introduce children to what it is like to fly in a plane.

Williams, John; *Air,* Wayland Publishers Ltd., 1990.
ISBN o-7502-0268-8
While looking at air and indicators that it is there, and machines that use air to make them work, this book is full of fun ideas for making windmills, wind wheels, kites, and parachutes.

Williams, John; *Flight,* Wayland Publishers Ltd., 1991,
ISBN 0-7502-0026-X
A book full of ideas for making paper darts, gliders, kites, helicopters and model birds. Notes are included on how this topic can be included in primary science and cross-curricular teaching.

TIME

Anno, Mitsumasa; *The Earth Is A Sundial,* The Bodley Head Ltd., 1984
ISBN 0-370-31016-0
A pop-up book with activities designed to use shadows to tell time.

Gibbons, Gail; *The Reasons For Seasons,* Holiday House, 1995.
ISBN 0-8234-1174-5
A pictorial explanation of how the position of the earth in relation to the sun causes our seasons and the wonders that come with them.

Humphrey, Henry and Deidre O'Meara Humphrey; *When Is Now?* Doubleday and Company Ltd., 1980.
ISBN 0-385-13215-8
A well-illustrated book to help children trace the development of time-keeping devices and to assist them in making their own models and to experiment with these devices.

Knapp, Brian; *Time,* Grolier Ltd., 1992.
ISBN 0-7172-2875-4
A structure of diagrams, text, and activities to give children an idea how time influences everything from our body clock to the origin of the universe.

Kurth, Heinz; *Time,* The Windmill Press, 1973.
ISBN 0-437-53605-X
Pictures and text look at some aspects of this mysterious medium called time. It shows how concepts of time have changed and progressed over the years.

Smith, A.G.; *What Time Is It?,* Stoddard Publishing Company Ltd., 1992.
ISBN 0-77375-525-X
A book filled with detailed illustrations of numerous timekeeping devices from every age; how calendars were invented; and how people kept track of time before clocks were used.

Webb, Angela; *Talk About Sand,* Franklin Watts Inc., 1992
ISBN 0-531-10370-6
A well-illustrated book that will challenge children to suggest ideas for exploration and experimentation with sand. Activities include making a timer.

Yorke, Jane (Ed.); *Time,* Random House, 1991.
ISBN 0-679-81164-8
A picture book with a first look at what happens in time from getting up in the morning to going to bed at night.

Zubrowski, Bernie; *Raceways: Having Fun With Balls And Tracks,* Greenwillow Books, 1985. Distributed by Gage Educational Publishing Co.
ISBN 0-688-04159-0
Using plastic decorative molding available in lumber supply stores, children can make marbles go up and down hills, travel in a circle, and jump from track to track without falling off. Travel times as well as basic scientific ideas such as energy, acceleration, and momentum can be linked to a variety of illustrated games and experiments to try.

Also of Interest to Teachers: